EDUCATIONAL

**ADVANCED
SUBSIDIARY**

Revise AS
Sociology

Author

Steve Chapman

Contents

Chapter 6 Religion

Chapter 7 Youth and culture

Chapter 8 Wealth, welfare and poverty

Chapter 9 Work and leisure

Chapter 10 Health

Specification lists

AQA Sociology

UNIT	SPECIFICATION TOPIC	CHAPTER REFERENCE	STUDIED IN CLASS	REVISED	PRACTICE QUESTIONS
Unit 1 _Family and households_	Family and state policy	2.1			
	Industrialisation and family change	2.2			
	Changing patterns of marriage, co-habitation and family breakdown	2.1			
	Household and family diversity	2.1			
	Gender, power and domestic labour	2.3			
	Children and childhood	2.3			
Unit 1 _Health_	Health as a social construct	10.1			
	Explanations for health inequalities	10.2			
	Inequalities in health care access and provision	10.3			
	Mental health and illness	10.1			
	Role of medicine and health professionals	10.3			
Unit 1 _Mass media_	Relationship between ownership and control	5.1			
	Relationship between mass media and ideology	5.1			
	Selection and presentation of media content	5.2, 5.3			
	Representations of age, social class, gender, ethnicity, etc.	5.3			
	Mass media and audiences	5.2			
Unit 2 _Education_	Role of education	3.2			
	Explanations for educational inequalities	3.3			
	Classroom interaction	3.3			
	Pupil sub-cultures	3.3			
	Hidden curriculum	3.2			
	State educational policy	3.1			

UNIT	SPECIFICATION TOPIC	CHAPTER REFERENCE	STUDIED IN CLASS	REVISED	PRACTICE QUESTIONS
Unit 2 Wealth, poverty and welfare	Definitions of poverty, wealth and income	8.1			
	Explanations for distribution of poverty and wealth	8.1			
	Explanations for poverty	8.1			
	Social policy responses to poverty	8.2			
	The nature and role of public, private, voluntary and informal welfare provision	8.2			
Unit 2 Work and organisations	Theories of management and organisation of work	9.1			
	Explanations for work satisfaction, alienation and conflict at work	9.1			
	Technological change	9.1			
	Causes and social effects of unemployment	9.2			
	Leisure and its impact on identity and consumption	9.2			
Unit 3 Sociological methods	Primary quantitative and qualitative methods	1.2			
	Survey questionnaires	1.2			
	Interviews	1.2			
	Observation techniques	1.2			
	Experiments	1.2			
	Secondary quantitative and qualitative methods	1.3			
	Relationship between theory and method	1.1			

Examination analysis

The specification comprises three examinations.

Unit 1	This unit is divided into three sections: Family and Households, Health, and Mass media. Each section contains one data response question. Candidates must choose one section and answer the question in it.	1 hr 15 min test 35%
Unit 2	This unit is divided into three sections: Education, Wealth, poverty and welfare, and Work and organisations. Each section contains one data response question. Candidates must choose one section and answer the question in it.	1 hr 15 min test 35%
Unit 3W OR	This unit contains one compulsory data response question on Sociological methods.	1 hr text 30%
Unit 3C	Coursework task	30%

OCR Sociology

UNIT	SPECIFICATION TOPIC	CHAPTER REFERENCE	STUDIED IN CLASS	REVISED	PRACTICE QUESTIONS
Unit 2532 The individual and society	Definitions	4.1			
	Socialisation	4.1			
	Identity	4.1			
	Theories of culture, socialisation and identity	4.1			
	Gender, masculinity and femininity	4.2			
	National identity	4.2			
	Ethnic identity	4.2			
	Class identity	4.2			
	Consumption and identity	4.2			
Unit 2533 Culture and socialisation	**The Family**				
	Family concepts and definitions	2.1			
	Recent demographic change	2.1			
	Social policy and the family	2.1			
	Diversity in families and households	2.1			
	Domestic power relations	2.3			
	Parents and children	2.3			
	Dark side of family life	2.3			
	Mass media				
	Ownership and control	5.1			
	News and moral panics	5.3			
	Media stereotyping: gender	5.3			
	Media stereotyping: ethnicity	5.3			
	Media stereotyping: class	5.3			
	Theories of media content	5.2			
	Effects of mass media	5.2			
	Religion				
	Religious institutions	6.1			
	Secularisation	6.2			
	Religion and control	6.3			
	Religion and classical sociology	6.3			

UNIT	SPECIFICATION TOPIC	CHAPTER REFERENCE	STUDIED IN CLASS	REVISED	PRACTICE QUESTIONS
Unit 2533 *Culture and socialisation*	**Youth and culture**				
	Theories of youth subcultures	7.1			
	Youth, social class, ethnicity and gender	7.1			
	Theories of juvenile delinquency	7.2			
	Impact of class, gender and ethnicity on experience of schooling	3.3			
	Subcultures in school	3.3			
	Femininity, masculinity and subject choice	3.3			
Unit 2534 *Sociological research skills*	Basic concepts	1.1			
	Sampling	1.2			
	Collecting primary data:				
	Surveys	1.2			
	Questionnaires	1.2			
	Interviews	1.2			
	Observation	1.2			
	Sources of secondary data	1.3			
	Interpreting and evaluating data	1.2			

Examination analysis

The specification comprises three examinations.

Unit 2532	Candidates choose one question from a choice of two structured questions.	1 hr test	30%
Unit 2533	Candidates must do two two-part structured essay questions chosen from the same or different options.	1 hr 30 min test	40%
Unit 2534 OR	One compulsory data response question on Sociological Research Skills.	1 hr test	30%
Unit 2534	Research Report		30%

AS/A2 Level Sociology courses

AS and A2

All Sociology A Level courses being studied from September 2000 are in two parts, with three separate modules in each part. Students first study the AS (Advanced Subsidiary) course. Some will then go on to study the second part of the A Level course, called A2. Advanced Subsidiary is assessed at the standard expected halfway through an A Level course: i.e. between GCSE and Advanced GCE. This means that new AS and A2 courses are designed so that difficulty steadily increases.

- However AS Sociology requires no prior learning or achievement at GCSE.
- A2 Sociology does naturally follow on from AS Sociology.

How will you be tested?

Assessment units

For AS Sociology, you will be tested by three assessment units. For the full A Level in Sociology, you will take a further three units. AS Sociology forms 50% of the assessment weighting for the full A Level.

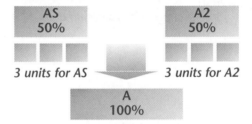

Each unit can normally be taken in either January or June. Alternatively, you can study the whole course before taking any of the unit examinations. There is a lot of flexibility about when exams can be taken and the diagram below shows just some of the ways that the assessment units may be taken for AS and A Level Sociology.

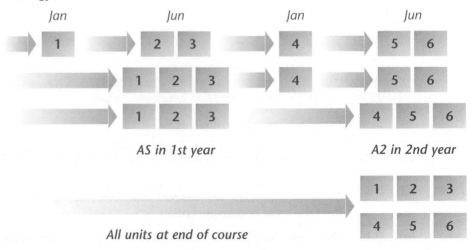

If you are disappointed with a module result, you can resit each module once. You will need to be very careful about when you take up a resit opportunity because you will only have one chance to improve your mark. The higher mark counts.

A2 and Synoptic assessment

After having studied AS Sociology, you may wish to continue studying Sociology to A Level. For this, you will need to take three further units of Sociology at A2. Similar assessment arrangements apply except some units, those that draw together different parts of the course in a 'synoptic' assessment have to be assessed at the end of the course.

Coursework

Coursework may form part of your A Level Sociology course as an alternative to Unit 3 (AQA) and Unit 2534 (OCR).

AQA offer students the option of a Coursework task at AS Level. Students are required to submit a Research Proposal which should be no more than 1200 words.

OCR offers students the option of a research report at AS Level. Students are required to write a report of no longer than 1000 words on a piece of sociological research that they have chosen.

Key skills

It is important that you develop your key skills throughout your AS and A2 courses. These are important skills that you need whatever you do beyond AS and A Levels. To gain the key skills qualification, which is the equivalent to a grade 'D' at A Level, you will need to collect evidence in a portfolio to show that you have attained Level 3 in Communication, Application of number and Information technology. You will also need to take a formal test in each key skill. You will have many opportunities during AS Sociology to develop your key skills.

It is a worthwhile qualification, as it demonstrates your ability to put your ideas across to other people, collect data and use up-to-date technology in your work.

What skills will I need?

For AS Sociology, you will be tested by assessment objectives: these are the skills that you should have acquired by studying the course. The assessment objectives for AS Sociology are shown below.

Knowledge and understanding

- Recall of theories, methods, concepts and various forms of evidence and the links between them.
- Understanding of theories, methods, concepts and evidence and the links between them.
- Clearly and effectively communicating sociological knowledge and understanding.

Identification, analysis, interpretation and evaluation

- Identification of facts, opinions and value judgements.
- Analysis and evaluation of the design of a range of investigations.
- Analysis and evaluation of the methods used to collect, select and record relevant evidence accurately.
- Selection and application of a range of relevant concepts and theories.
- Interpretation of quantitative and qualitative data.
- Identification and evaluation of significant social trends.
- Evaluation of different theories, arguments and evidence.

Different types of questions in AS examinations

In AS Sociology examinations, different types of question are used to assess your abilities and skills.

Data response questions

All questions for the AQA AS Level specifications are data response questions. Generally you will be given two pieces of data. These are known as Items A and B and are likely to be in the form of text, graphs, charts etc. Data response questions are organised in six parts with marks progressing upwards 2, 4, 6, 8, 20 and 20. These parts are directly or indirectly related to the Items.

The organisation of data response questions in Units 1 and 2 is fairly predictable and the format will generally tend to follow this pattern;

(a) 'Explain what is meant by' followed by a sociological term.

(b) Suggest or identify two factors, examples, differences, ways, etc.

(c) Suggest three ways, etc.

(d) Identify and briefly describe, explain, discuss, etc.

Parts (e) and (f) are short essays worth 20 marks each. It is important to devote as much time to each of these as you have done to the section a–d. Often these questions will ask you to use material from the Items in your essay. If you ignore this instruction, you will not be able to gain full marks.

Unit 3 of the AQA AS Level specifications has a slightly different variation on the data response question. You will be given three Items of information and the format of questions will follow this pattern:

(a) You will be asked for the 'name given to' a particular sociological method described in the question for 1 mark.

(b) This question may be in two or three parts and will ask you to examine a piece of data associated with a piece of research. You are likely to be asked to identify the method used and problems associated with the research. This will be worth 5 marks.

(c) This question will be in two or three parts and will ask questions relating to another one of the Items, e.g. you may be asked to explain what is meant by sociological terms used in the Item. This will be worth 6 marks.

(d) For 8 marks, you will be put into a specific research situation (e.g. research on boys' behaviour in schools) and asked to identify and explain two practical problems.

Parts (e) and (f) are short essays worth 20 marks each. As in the Units 1 and 2, it is important to devote as much time to each of these as you do to parts a–d. These questions are also likely to ask you to specifically use the information in the Items and/or to use studies with which you are familiar. If you ignore these instructions, you will not be able to gain full marks.

Many of the practice questions in this book are AQA-type data response questions.

Unit 2532 of the OCR AS Level specifications also assesses using a data response question but this is different in format to the AQA versions. You will be given a piece of data which may be in the form of text, photographs, graph, chart, etc. The question is organised into four parts with marks progressing 12, 12, 26 and 40.

These parts are directly or indirectly related to the Item.

The organisation of this data response is fairly predictable and the format will generally tend to follow this pattern:

(a) Identify and/or briefly explain the meaning or function of a sociological term or concept used in the Item for 12 marks.

(b) Identify and briefly explain two ways, trends, examples of a sociological process, etc. for 12 marks.

(c) Outline and comment on two ways in which a sociological process occurs for 26 marks.

Part (d) is a short essay asking you to 'discuss' a particular issue relating to the individual and society.

The practice question in chapter 4 is a working example of this type of question.

Structured essay questions

OCR Unit 2533 Culture and Socialisation offers you a choice of structured essay questions. These are organised into two parts. Part (a) will ask you to 'identify and explain two ways, aspects, differences, etc. of a sociological problem relating to the option for 20 marks. Part (b) is an essay question asking you to 'outline and discuss a view' relating to the option for 40 marks.

Some of the practice questions in this book take this format.

Research questions

OCR Unit 2534 Sociological Research Skills is a combination of essay and data response questions. You will be given two pieces of information. Item A is likely to be a proposal for a research design. Question part (a) will ask you to define a key term or concept used in that design for 8 marks whereas part (b) will ask you 'identify and explain the main weaknesses of the research design' for 35 marks. Question part (c) will ask you to summarise in your own words quantitative or qualitative data contained in Item B for 14 marks. Part (d) is an essay question asking you to 'outline in detail and briefly assess' a method that could have been used to research the data in Item B.

A practice question in this format can be found in Chapter 1.

Exam technique

Links from GCSE

AS Sociology requires no prior learning or achievement at GCSE although it is useful to have a grade 'C' in GCSE English Language because of the emphasis on essay writing.

What are examiners looking for?

Examiners use instructions to help you to decide the length and depth of your answer. In essays and data response questions the following 'action' or 'trigger' words and phrases are frequently used.

State, define, what is meant by, name

These normally require a short, concise answer and is often recall material that can be learned by rote.

Explain, discuss

Some reasoning or some reference to theory is required. It normally involves reference to both sides of a debate.

Outline, describe

This implies a short response which sums up the major points of one particular theory or approach.

Identify, suggest, illustrate

These words normally require you to apply your knowledge to a particular sociological problem or theory.

Assess, examine, evaluate

These words suggest that you should look at the strengths and weaknesses of an argument or both sides of a particular debate. You should offer judgement based on evidence.

Some dos and don'ts

Do read the rubric, i.e. the set of instructions at the start of the exam paper.

You don't want to answer too many questions or not enough or answer from the wrong sections.

Do answer the question set rather than the one you wished was set.

Do spend 5 minutes reading through the Items and the questions.

It is especially important to read through all the questions before attempting any of them. A common mistake is to use information to answer a question which is more appropriate to another question.

Do plan your response to any question worth over 20 marks.

Do pay special attention to the way marks are divided up between sections of data responses.

It is wasteful to write more than is required and it will impact negatively on the time left for the bigger questions.

Do always clearly label the part of the question you are answering.

Do use the data provided in the Items whenever it is relevant to do so.

Respond to the appropriate 'action' words and phrases. Failure to use them could result in you failing to pick up marks.

Do exercise care when it comes to the interpretation of statistics, tables and diagrams especially in regard to scale.

Marks are easily wasted because the candidate fails to look at how the data is organised (i.e. into percentages, thousands, etc.).

Do take care in how you present sociological thinkers and theory.

You need to recognise that contributions to sociological debate are a product of a specific time and place. For example, try to avoid suggesting that 19th-century sociologists are still making a regular contribution to modern sociological debate.

Do take notice of 'action' words and phrases such as 'contemporary', 'recently', 'post Second World War', 'last twenty years', etc.

These words want you to set your response in a modern context. Any reference to studies and debate outside these periods (e.g. 'contemporary' and 'recent' usually mean the last 20 years) will be regarded as largely irrelevant to the question. It is not necessary to know the exact date of a study but do know the decade in which it was produced.

Do make your sociology more valid by being aware of current social and political events.

Be aware of how sociological theory and methods can be applied to them. Examiners want you to be able to apply your knowledge to the real world and its social problems.

Do take care with regard to grammar and spelling.

Poor grammatical structure and spelling can impair the intelligibility of a response or weaken the argument used. A coherent and logical presentation of argument and evidence is necessary to achieve a good AS Level standard.

Don't waste time writing out the question.

This wastes time. The marks are for the answer.

Don't mistake your own opinion for sociology.

Try and back up what you say with evidence.

Don't over-simplify sociological debate by presenting ideological positions as irreconcilable.

Examiners are concerned that functionalists and positivists are often presented as 'bad' sociologists whilst Marxists and interpretivists are seen as 'good' sociologists. You need to demonstrate that sociological studies which seem opposed actually share common research problems and theoretical underpinnings. In other words, similarities are just as important as differences. This is comparing and contrasting.

Don't over-rely on pre-prepared 'shopping list' answers.

Try to avoid writing down all you know about a particular area, regardless of the question asked.

Be prepared to be flexible and to adapt your knowledge to the question set. Think on your feet. There are no rehearsed or model answers.

Don't be one-sided in your evaluation.

Don't focus disproportionately on the virtues of a debate, theory or method at the expense of its drawbacks or vice versa. In order to get into the higher mark bands, your evaluation must be balanced.

What grade do you want?

Everyone would like to improve their grades but you will only manage this with a lot of hard work and determination. You should have a fair idea of your natural ability and likely grade in Sociology and the hints below offer advice on improving that grade.

For a Grade A

You will need to be a very good all-rounder.

- You must go into every exam knowing the work extremely well.
- You must be able to apply your knowledge to new, unfamiliar situations.
- You need to have practised many, many exam questions so that you are ready for the type of question that will appear.

The exams test all areas of the syllabus and any weaknesses in your sociology will be found out. There must be no holes in your knowledge and understanding. For a Grade A, you must be competent in all areas.

For a Grade C

You must have a reasonable grasp of Sociology but you may have weaknesses in several areas and you will be unsure of sociological concepts and theories.

- Many Grade C candidates are just as good at answering questions as the Grade A students but holes and weaknesses often show up in just some topics.
- To improve, you will need to master your weaknesses and you must prepare thoroughly for the exam. You must become a better all-rounder.

For a Grade E

You cannot afford to miss the easy marks. Even if you find Sociology difficult to understand and would be happy with a Grade E, there are plenty of questions in which you can gain marks.

- You must memorise all definitions and basic concepts.
- You must practise exam questions to give yourself confidence that you do know some Sociology. In exams, answer the parts of questions that you know first. You must not waste time on the difficult parts. You can always go back to these later.
- The areas of Sociology that you find most difficult are going to be hard to score on in exams. Even in the difficult questions, there are still marks to be gained.

The table below shows how your average mark is translated:

average	80%	70%	60%	50%	40%
grade	A	B	C	D	E

You can always gain some marks if you only partly outline a theory or sociological response to a problem. If it is a data response question, you can pick up marks by fully using the data.

Four steps to successful revision

Step 1: Understand

- Study the topic to be learned slowly. Make sure you understand the logic or important concepts.
- Mark up the text if necessary – underline, highlight and make notes
- Re-read each paragraph slowly.

GO TO STEP 2

Step 2: Summarise

- Now make your own revision note summary:
  What is the main idea, theme or concept to be learned?
  What are the main points? How does the logic develop?
  Ask questions: Why? How? What next?
- Use bullet points, mind maps, patterned notes.
- Link ideas with mnemonics, mind maps, crazy stories.
- Note the title and date of the revision notes
  (e.g. Sociology: Family diversity, 3rd March).
- Organise your notes carefully and keep them in a file.

This is now in short-term memory. You will forget 80% of it if you do not go to Step 3. GO TO STEP 3, but first take a 10 minute break.

Step 3: Memorise

- Take 25 minute learning 'bites' with 5 minute breaks.
- After each 5 minute break test yourself:
  Cover the original revision note summary
  Write down the main points
  Speak out loud (record on tape)
  Tell someone else
  Repeat many times.

The material is well on its way to long-term memory. You will forget 40% if you do not do step 4. GO TO STEP 4

Step 4: Track/Review

- Create a Revision Diary (one A4 page per day).
- Make a revision plan for the topic, e.g. 1 day later, 1 week later, 1 month later.
- Record your revision in your Revision Diary, e.g.
  Sociology: Family diversity, 3rd March 25 minutes
  Sociology: Family diversity, 5th March 15 minutes
  Sociology: Family diversity, 3rd April 15 minutes
  ... and then at monthly intervals.

Chapter 1

Research methods

The following topics are covered in this chapter:

- *The relationship between theory and methods*
- *Primary data collection*
- *Secondary research methods*

1.1 The relationship between theory and methods

After studying this section you should be able to:

- *define the key concepts of reliability, validity, objectivity and representativeness*
- *outline the relationship between theory and methods*
- *identify the theoretical, practical and ethical considerations influencing sociological research*

LEARNING SUMMARY

Key concepts

| AQA | U 3 |
| OCR | U 2534 |

Examiners often ask the meaning of these words. Know them well!

A research method is said to have high **reliability** if another researcher is able to repeat the study exactly and obtain the same results. **Objectivity** refers to the ability to be open-minded and free from personal or political bias. The data or evidence collected by a particular method has **validity** for sociologists if it accurately reflects the reality of those being studied. **Representativeness** refers to whether the group being studied is typical of the larger group to which the sociologist thinks they belong. If this is the case, the sociologist can **generalise** their findings to the larger group.

The debate between positivist and interpretivist sociology

| AQA | U 3 |
| OCR | U2534 |

Traditionally, a sociologist's choice of research method depended on whether they subscribed to a **positivist** or **interpretivist** view of society.

An excellent example of this in practice is Durkheim's study of suicide.

Positivism

KEY POINT

- Positivists believe that only science can provide the objective 'truth' or facts about the world.
- Positivist sociologists believe that human behaviour is determined by social forces beyond the control of society's members. These forces are generally referred to as 'laws' or 'social facts'. Positivists claim these are the product of the way in which societies are organised.
- Positivist sociologists therefore believe that sociology should be a scientific discipline based on the logic and methods of the natural sciences. The job of sociologists is to uncover the social laws that govern human behaviour.

When positivists collect information about the social world, they usually subscribe to a scientific model known as **the hypothetico-deductive approach**. This is the model that natural science employs in, for example, **laboratory experiments**.

Stage 1 Phenomena are observed.

Stage 2 A testable hypothesis (an educated guess) is constructed to explain the phenomena.

Empirical = collection of facts and observations

Stage 3 Empirical data (factual information) is collected in a systematic way.

Stage 4 The data is interpreted and analysed to see whether it confirms or refutes the hypothesis.

Stage 5 If the hypothesis is confirmed time and time again, it becomes a theory. If the data refutes the hypothesis, the scientist should reject or revise it, and begin the data-collection process again.

The major scientific method in the natural sciences used for collecting data is the laboratory experiment. In Sociology, the major scientific method used by positivists is the social or sample survey, which incorporates the use of the questionnaire and/or structured interview. Positivists also advocate the use of some types of secondary data, particularly official statistics.

The interpretivist critique of positivism

Examiners sometimes refer to Interpretivists as Phenomenologists!

KEY POINT

- Interpretivist (anti-positivist) sociologists are sceptical about sociology's scientific status. They argue that human behaviour is not the result of external social laws. Society is the product of interaction – meaning when people come together in social groups. The way people interpret these social interactions is centrally important to the understanding of social behaviour.

Verstehen = empathy with people's actions

- Interpretivists prefer methods such as unstructured interviews and observation because these uncover the meanings behind action and emphasise validity. Such methods attempt to see the social world through the eyes of the people who inhabit it by studying their everyday life (*verstehen*) or by letting those being studied speak for themselves.

Practical constraints on choice of method

In addition to the theoretical, there are also practical reasons why a particular research method might be chosen.

- Funding – if the sociologist does not have access to large funds, a cheap method will be required. Secondary data is cheap because it has already been collected. Postal questionnaires are cheaper than interviews, which are probably cheaper than observation studies.

- Time – if you have years, observation may be possible. However if you only have months, you need a method that results in a quick response like questionnaires and/or interviews.

Think of practical examples to illustrate these points in an exam!

- The subject matter is going to influence choice of research. For example, research into trends may suit quantitative research whilst research into attitudes may suit qualitative methods.

- The research population may not be accessible because it is regarded as deviant and may feel threatened. If this is the case, covert observation may be necessary.

- The research population may be geographically dispersed. If it is, a postal questionnaire may be necessary, especially if money is tight.

Ethical considerations

Some methods experience more ethical problems than others e.g. covert observations.

There are some generally agreed professional guidelines which are followed in social research. For example:

- Subjects should not have their physical, social and psychological well-being adversely affected by research.

- Research should be based on the freely given, informed consent of those being studied.

- Research should not involve an intrusion on privacy, and research subjects should be allowed anonymity and confidentiality if they so wish.

Progress check

1 Which sociological theory claims that human behaviour is the product of social forces beyond our control?

2 What is 'empirical' data?

3 What method is normally employed by natural scientists to collect empirical data?

4 By what other names are interpretivist sociologists also known?

5 What does 'verstehen' mean and which theory is it associated with?

5 Empathetic understanding or seeing the world through the eyes of those being studied. Interpretivism.
4 Anti-positivists or phenomenologists.
3 The laboratory experiment.
2 That which is collected by practical research.
1 Positivism.

1.2 Primary data collection

After studying this section you should be able to:

- *describe different types of primary research methods and distinguish between quantitative and qualitative types of research*
- *identify the strengths and limitations of different sources of primary data and methods of research*

LEARNING SUMMARY

What is primary data?

AQA   U3
OCR   U2534

Primary data is that which is collected by sociologists themselves during their own research using research tools such as experiments, survey questionnaires, interviews and observation.

KEY POINT

This advice is essential when analysing tables, graphs, etc. if you are not to lose marks.

Primary data can take a **quantitative** or statistical form, e.g. charts, graphs, diagrams and tables. It is essential to interpret and evaluate this type of data with care. In particular, look at how the data is organised in terms of **scale**. Is it organised into percentages, hundreds, thousands, etc.? Is it a snapshot of a particular year or is it focusing on trends across a number of years?

Primary data can also be **qualitative**, e.g. extracts from the conversations of those being studied. Some researchers present their arguments virtually entirely in the words of their subject matter. Consequently the data speaks for itself and readers are encouraged to make their own judgements.

The experimental method

Used more by psychologists than sociologists, e.g. see Milgram, Zimbardo.

This is the main method used by natural scientists. Experimentation normally involves the testing of a hypothesis about the relationship between an independent variable (cause) and a dependent variable (effect). Experiments are usually set up so that the scientist controls the introduction of possible independent variables. In the natural sciences, such control is enhanced by use of a laboratory. Any change in the participant's behaviour should be the result of the change introduced by the experimenter. Interpretivist sociologists note that the experimental method is rarely used in sociological research for both practical and ethical reasons:

- **Practical reasons:** Sociologists can never be sure that behaviour is caused by the social phenomena they are interested in. For example, people usually know they are taking part in an experiment. Their performance may be distorted by their desire to impress the experimenter. Moreover, only a limited number of social conditions can be re-created in the laboratory.

E.g. media research on children, see Bandura.

- **Ethical reasons:** Some sociologists argue that it is morally wrong not to tell people they are part of an experiment or to expose them to adverse social conditions.

These difficulties have led to some sociologists adopting variations on the experimental method. The **comparative method** is an experimental method which uses the social world as the laboratory. The researcher, usually using official statistics, compares a **before and after** situation in a social group where a change has taken place with one where it has not.

I.e. Durkheim's suicide.

Interpretivist sociologists have used **field experiments** – a qualitative examination of particular social contexts in order to explore the interpretations which underpin everyday interaction. However, these too involve some degree of manipulation. Positivists note that this type of experiment may suffer lower levels of reliability.

I.e. Rosenthal and Jacobson.

The social survey

This is the method most favoured by positivist sociologists. It normally involves the random selection of a sample which is representative of the population the sociologist is interested in studying. This sample may be sent standardised questionnaires through the post and/or may be asked to take part in structured interviews.

Sometimes called the sample survey.

> **KEY POINT**
> The social survey normally results in the obtaining of large amounts of quantitative data in a relatively short period of time.

Sampling

Electoral registers are the most common sampling frames.

The selected sample must be **representative** of the population being studied because normally sociologists wish to **generalise**. It is also important to find a **sampling frame** (a list of people who may potentially take part in a survey) which is representative of the **population being studied**. Sociologists prefer to use **random sampling** methods in order to minimise the possibility of **bias**. At its most basic, random sampling allows everyone the same chance of being selected. A number of sampling methods are available to sociologists:

- **Systematic sampling:** Every nth person is chosen from a sampling frame. For example, 50 people out of a group of 500 may be chosen by randomly selecting a number between 1 and 10, e.g. 6. Every tenth name beginning with the randomly selected number '6' is taken from the list, e.g. 6, 16, 26, 36, 46... up to 496. This process will generate fifty names for the sample.

- Stratified sampling: A random sample is taken from particular social categories, e.g. age, gender, race, etc., which make up the population being studied.
- Cluster or multi-stage sampling: Households may be randomly selected from a random sample of streets from a random selection of areas.

Sometimes non-random and unrepresentative sampling methods may be preferred despite the danger of unreliability:

- Quota sampling is mainly used by market researchers in the street. For example, they may be under instructions to stop and interview a quota of housewives aged between 25 and 40 years of age.
- Snowball, or opportunity, sampling is mainly used in areas in which it is difficult to find a sample because behaviour is seen as deviant by society, e.g. a researcher interested in heroin addiction may find an addict willing to introduce him or her to other addicts.

E.g. the Census.

> **KEY POINT**
>
> Positivists approve of the social survey because it is regarded as scientific (variables are controlled via sampling and questionnaire design), reliable (standardised questionnaires can be replicated), objective (samples are randomly selected) and quantifiable. However, some social groups are difficult (and sometimes impossible) to survey, e.g. people who are illiterate and criminals.

I.e. the T.V. series '7-up' and 'Citizen 2000'.

Surveys which monitor a group over a period of years are called longitudinal surveys. They supply an in-depth picture of a group or social trends over time. Trust can be built up between a group and the researchers. This may generate more valid data and lessen the possibility of non-response. However, it can be difficult to find samples and research teams committed to long-term research. The sample may drop out, die, move away, etc. This increases the chance of it being unrepresentative. If different researchers are used, it can be difficult to re-establish trust with a group. The sample may become too 'survey-friendly'. They may consciously or unconsciously tell researchers what they want to hear.

The postal questionnaire

AQA — U3
OCR — U2534

Most social surveys use a postal questionnaire. These can be closed, meaning that respondents are normally given a fixed number of responses to tick. Some questionnaires use open-ended questions, especially attitude surveys. The postal questionnaire has particular advantages. It is cheap – especially if the sample is large or geographically scattered. It can use larger samples than any other method. It is reasonably quick in that the bulk of returned questionnaires are usually back within a month. Questionnaires that use closed questions are customer-friendly and easily quantified.

The *Hite Report into Sexual Behaviour* only had a 3% response rate!

However, the postal questionnaire suffers from a number of potential problems. A low response rate may call into question the representativeness of the sample. Researchers can never be sure the right person filled it in. It is inflexible because there is usually no opportunity to probe or observe the social context in which questions are answered. They can only be considered when questions are simple and straightforward. Question design is not easy, e.g. leading and ambiguous questions must be avoided because they undermine objectivity and introduce bias.

> **KEY POINT**
>
> Interpretivists don't like them because both the questions and fixed responses reflect what the sociologist thinks is important. Closed questions don't allow people to speak for themselves, and don't allow for the fact that, although people may share similar views, their reasons for doing so may be different.

Types of interview

AQA   U3
OCR   U2534

The structured interview

Always be willing to illustrate with examples, e.g. Wilmott and Young *Family and Kinship in East London.*

> **KEY POINT**
>
> The structured or formal interview involves the researcher working through a questionnaire or interview schedule as part of a social survey. Like the postal questionnaire, all respondents are exposed to the same set of questions.

Positivists like this type of interview because:

- They produce large amounts of factual information very cheaply and quickly compared with the unstructured interview and observation.

- An interviewer can explain the questionnaire, thus reducing the possibility of non-response and ask for clarification of vague responses.

- An interviewer can observe the social context in which answers are given, e.g. the facial expression, tone of voice, body language, status, etc., of the respondent.

The unstructured interview

Examples include, *Schooling the Smash St. Kids* by Paul Corrigan *and Learning to Labour* by Paul Willis.

> **KEY POINT**
>
> Interpretivists argue that research should focus on the respondent's view of the world through the use of unstructured interviews (sometimes known as 'guided conversations'). This method involves the interviewer informally asking open-ended questions about a topic and allowing the respondent to respond freely and in depth.

Interpretivists claim a number of strengths for this method:

- Trust can be developed, which may generate more qualitative information about the respondent's interpretation of the world.

- They are flexible because the conversation is not constrained by fixed questions. This may generate more valid information (especially if the respondent can see their input is valued) and allows for probing of deeper meanings.

- They provide more opportunity for respondents to say what they want rather than what the interviewer expects.

However, positivists see this method as unscientific because it isn't standardised and doesn't produce quantifiable data. It depends upon a unique relationship between interviewer and interviewee and is therefore difficult to replicate.

Examiners like to see illustration of how bias might be caused by status differences!

> **KEY POINT**
>
> Both structured and unstructured interviews share similar potential problems. The major problem is **interview bias or effect**. People may not act naturally in interviews because all interviews are interaction situations and may be adversely affected by status differences between the interviewer and interviewee, e.g. social class, gender, ethnicity and age. Bias may be caused by the interviewer's facial expression or tone of voice, leading the interviewee to a response that reflects the interviewer's own opinions. A social desirability effect may occur in that the interviewee may wish to please the interviewer.

Interviews only provide a snapshot of social life whereas other methods such as observation may better capture everyday life. Interviews may be ineffective if people are unaware of behaving in the way they do.

Observation studies

AQA   U3
OCR   U2534

Ethnographic studies describe the way of life of a group of people from their point of view and so appeal most to interpretivist sociologists.

> **Observation** is the main type of ethnographic approach. There are four main types.
>
> - **External observation** involves an observer objectively viewing a group but not taking any part in their activities, e.g. classroom observation.
> - **Non-participant covert observation** involves secretly observing a group, e.g. through a one-way mirror.
> - **Participant observation** involves the sociologist joining the everyday routines of a group and observing action in its natural context. Those being observed have given their permission and are aware of the research aims.
> - **Covert observation** involves the sociologist concealing their identity and totally immersing themselves in a group culture.
>
> **KEY POINT**

Examiners like to see studies quoted. See Bill Whyte, James Patrick.

Interpretivists see observation as having a number of advantages:

- It is naturalistic – people are observed as they follow their everyday routine. The sociologist sees life through their eyes.
- The rapport established between the sociologist and the social group may produce more valid data.
- Participant observation can uncover behaviour and attitudes that people may be unaware of.

> Covert observation is good for studying deviant/criminal groups or groups that feel threatened. It is especially useful when participant observation would disturb natural rhythms and create artificial behaviour.
>
> **KEY POINT**

Positivists claim observation studies are unscientific.

- The presence of outsiders may influence the behaviour of the group observed – creating less valid data.
- The researcher may 'go native', i.e. become over-involved and lose detachment. Observers may see only what they want to see.
- Observation is not replicable. The same quality of relationship may not be established with another observer. The method is therefore unreliable.
- Observation is rarely quantified.
- It is difficult to generalise from observation studies because they focus on small samples – many of which are exotic and unrepresentative of mainstream society.

Impress the examiner! Show how Humphreys quantified his observations.

Observation may be impossible in some social situations because of differences in status. Observation may generate moral problems such as breaking the law, e.g. covert observation is seen by some as violating the principles of informed consent. Observation studies are time-consuming and costly. There are also practical problems in writing up notes without causing artificiality or without arousing suspicion if covert.

Should friendship be turned into data? Ethics?

However, interpretivists argue that these problems of reliability are made up for by the validity of the information produced.

23

Progress check

1 Cause and effect is the relationship between which two variables?

2 Why is it important to use random sampling methods?

3 What sampling method is best suited to the study of deviants?

4 Why is it important to get a good response rate to questionnaires?

5 What major problem is caused by the fact that interviews involve interaction?

6 What is ethnography?

6 The study of people in their everyday environments.
5 Interview bias or effect.
4 In order that the sample be representative of the population that is being studied.
3 Snowball sampling.
2 To minimise the possibility of bias and to obtain a representative sample from which generalisations can be made.
1 Independent (cause) and Dependent (effect).

1.3 Secondary research methods

After studying this section you should be able to:

- describe different types of secondary research methods and distinguish between quantitative and qualitative types of research
- identify the strengths and limitations of different sources of secondary data and methods of research

LEARNING SUMMARY

What is secondary data?

AQA U3
OCR U2534

> **KEY POINT**
>
> Secondary data is that produced by agencies other than the sociologist doing the research. For example, a sociologist studying joy-riding will try to read all other sociological literature on this topic. Secondary data is also produced by agencies such as the government, the mass media and private individuals.

Sources of secondary data

AQA U3
OCR U2534

Official statistics

This mainly refers to data already collected by governments, e.g. statistics relating to births, marriages, deaths, health, crime, the economy, etc. Official statistics are seen as scientific because they are collected in a highly standardised way. For example, some data has to be registered by law. Government surveys such as the Census, the General Household Survey and the British Crime Survey are viewed as highly reliable and objective in their design and execution.

Positivist sociologists suggest that official statistics are useful to sociologists because they are already available. Their use saves time, effort and money. They give a wide-ranging picture of social phenomenon. They have excellent comparative value in that they allow examination of trends over time.

Illustrate with reference to crime or divorce.

Interpretivists however, are very critical of statistics because they have been collected for non-sociological purposes. They may not include data in which the sociologist is interested or may be based on definitions which sociologists don't accept. They may be socially constructed and therefore tell us more about the people who collect them than about the social phenomena in question.

Mass media reports

Sociologists have used newspaper and magazine articles, television programmes, advertisements and films as sources of secondary data. In particular, interpretivist sociologists have used newspaper reports to give insight into past events and social concerns. The sociology of moral panics is one such area.

Some sociologists use content analysis to systematically analyse the content and meaning of media messages. Positivists have generally focused on breaking down the content of media into quantifiable categories, while interpretivists have attempted to 'read' the symbolic meaning of media messages – a type of analysis called semiology.

Analysis of mass media is relatively cheap because such reports are already available. Samples of people are not necessary. Content analysis is repeatable if used in its simple category form. It is allegedly objective because it does not interfere with what is being researched. It results in quantitative data.

However, its scientific status has been questioned by positivists. It can be very subjective and the same content may be interpreted in different ways by different sociologists. The method also implicitly assumes that the media have an impact on the audience of lasting significance. The evidence for this is mixed and certainly not proven. Content analysis rarely asks the audience what it thinks and assumes that the audience reacts in the same way. Media content may tell us more about the values and attitudes of journalists than those of society.

> Feminist analysis of media.

Historical documents

Historical documents such as government reports and white papers, historical treatises, diaries and even novels from a particular period may add qualitative insight into social problems. However, the reliability and validity of any historical document should be assessed by asking four key questions:

> Examiners like examples, e.g. Dickens, Austen, Hitler diaries.

KEY POINT

- How authentic is it?
- Does it have credibility? Might it involve exaggeration, deception and justification leading to bias?
- Is the document representative or typical? Documents such as diaries may only represent the views of an articulate minority and provide a selective picture of society.
- Do we share the author's interpretations?

Personal documents

These are documents such as diaries, letters, autobiographies and biographies. Sociologists may even examine photographs and the inscription on gravestones. Some sociologists ask people taking part in their research to keep a diary documenting activities and feelings. This is known as time-budgeting. However, all these methods may be too subjective. People may be more concerned with justifying their activities than objectively recounting their experiences.

> In Oakley's study, housewives kept diaries.

Towards a synthesis of primary and secondary research methods

AQA	U3
OCR	U2534

The 1980s and 1990s have seen sociologists taking a pragmatic view when it comes to choice of methods. Many now use a combination of quantitative and qualitative methods. For these sociologists 'what works best is best'. Consequently, what Morgan calls 'the theory war' may now be coming to an end.

Triangulation

> Example to use in the exam? Barker's study of the Moonies.

In the 1990s sociologists tend to use either triangulation or methodological pluralism. This is the use of more than one method of research in order to assess the validity of the data produced. It has a number of advantages:

> Questions which focus on strengths and weaknesses of particular methods should be concluded with reference to the need for this type of approach to research.

KEY POINT

- It can be used to check on the accuracy of the data gathered by each method.
- Qualitative research, e.g. unstructured interviews, can produce hypotheses which can be checked using quantitative methods such as the social survey.
- The two approaches can give a more complete and in-depth picture of the group being studied in the form of a case study.
- Qualitative research can explain and illustrate the reasons and motives for the patterns and trends uncovered by statistics.

However, triangulation can be expensive. It can produce vast amounts of data which can be difficult to analyse.

Progress check

1 Why do divorce statistics only give sociologists a partial picture of marital breakdown?

2 Why are unemployment statistics problematical?

3 Why don't positivists like semiological analysis of media content?

4 Which sociological approach most favours the use of documents, diaries and letters?

5 What is the name of the approach which combines both quantitative and qualitative methods?

5 Triangulation.
4 Interpretivism.
3 It is not seen as an objective method because sociologists subjectively interpret content according to categories they have chosen.
2 Because governments frequently change the rules as to which groups should be included.
1 They don't include separations and empty shell marriages.

Sample question and model answer

A typical AQA question.

Item A

There are a number of key concepts involved in survey work. 'Sampling' is the process by which a small, but representative group is chosen from the population. With all surveys there may be a problem of non-response. For example, people in your sample may refuse to fill in the questionnaire. If you wish to achieve a high response rate, it is suggested that you make your questionnaire anonymous. Second, keep your questionnaire short so that it does not take a lot of time to fill in. Third, wait while people complete the questions or write the answers in for them.

Item B

Quantitative methods are associated with a scientific approach. Social surveys are the major method of quantitative research and are carried out when a researcher wishes to gain statistical information from a large number of people. Normally the researcher wishes to make generalisations about the population as a whole. Questions are standardised. Everyone is asked the same questions in the same order. It is therefore assumed that people's responses are comparable since they are responding to exactly the same questions. The results of such methods are usually presented in the form of statistical tables, pie-charts and graphs.

Item C

Observation studies are the most important type of ethnographic research. However, this method is strongly dependent on the social characteristics of the observer. For example, most sociologists tend to be a good deal older than the pupils and students they intend to research. This may a problem because the young may be reluctant to 'open up' to older researchers. Covert observation is obviously out of the question. Sociologists such as Parker, Willis, Pryce and Corrigan were at an advantage because they were only in their early twenties when carrying out their research. However, even at this age, researchers may still have problems in seeing the world from the point of view of an eleven-year-old.

a) What is the name given to sociologists who are 'associated with a scientific approach'? (Item B) [1 mark]

One word answers are fine for one mark.

a) Positivists.

b) With reference to Item A:

   (i) explain what is meant by a 'representative group' [2 marks]

   (ii) identify two disadvantages that might arise from adopting the suggestions in Item A. [4 marks]

Don't over respond to questions worth 2–4 marks.

b) (i) This is a sample of people who strongly resemble the population that is being studied by the sociologist in terms of their social class, gender, age, etc. make-up.

   (ii) Any two from:

   • Anonymity makes it difficult for a researcher to go back to a respondent for further information or to assess the social context in which the response was made.

   • A short questionnaire probably involves closed questions with fixed multiple-choice responses. This is good for generating quantitative information but not for producing qualitative information, e.g. attitudes and feelings. For example, people may respond in the same

Sample question and model answer (continued)

way to questions but may do so for different motives which may not be spotted by a short questionnaire.

- The limited range of answers available in a short questionnaire may result in the sociologist imposing his or her feelings and ideas on the respondents.

- People may feel embarrassed or rushed if you wait for them to fill in a questionnaire or if you fill it in for them – especially if the subject matter of the questionnaire is sensitive. This may reduce the validity of the information generated.

c) With reference to Item C:

(i) what is meant by the term 'ethnographic research'? [2 marks]

> **Questions worth 2 marks should produce one or two sentence responses only.**

c) (i) This is research which observes a social group in its everyday, natural environment. For example, Bill Whyte's Street Corner Society (1943).

(ii) identify a social characteristic other than age which might make it difficult for some sociologists to conduct research in schools [2 marks]

(ii) Any from the following: gender, social class, race.

(iii) explain what is meant by 'covert observation' [2 marks]

(iii) This involves joining a social group incognito. Nobody knows you are a sociologist.

> **The model identifies several problems but you must also explain why these are problems.**

(iv) identify and briefly explain one practical problem and one ethical problem that might arise when studying football violence by means of covert participant observation. [8 marks]

(iv) Practical problems might include having the social and physical characteristics to be accepted without suspicion into a violent group, maintaining a convincing role without recourse to violent action, maintaining personal safety, avoiding arrest, writing notes without attracting attention and leaving the group without attracting reprisal/retaliation.

Ethical problems include the possibility of being involved in violent and criminal actions, encouraging or condoning actions which may lead to harm to others and using personal friendship for personal gain, i.e. a sociological study.

d) Using material from the Items and elsewhere, discuss the strengths and weaknesses of the social survey. [20 marks]

> **The question explicitly asks you to use the material in the Items. If you ignore it you will not pick up all the marks on offer.**

d) As Item B points out, the social survey is the main method of quantitative research. Social surveys usually take the form of standardised postal questionnaires or structured interviews. The questionnaire in both these forms is aimed at a selected representative sample of the population. Social surveys are usually carried out when a researcher wishes to make generalisations about sections of society. As Item B notes, positivist sociologists see social surveys as scientific and reliable because they are easily replicated and their findings checked and verified.

The postal questionnaire is seen as particularly advantageous because it is

Sample question and model answer (continued)

relatively cheap and it can use larger, more geographically dispersed samples. However, as Item A notes, non-response can be a major problem. In some past surveys it has fallen below 50%, e.g. The Hite Report had a 3% response rate. Non-response can be reduced through the use of structured interviews. The interviewer can make sure that the questionnaire is fully explained and understood. However, the validity of interview data can be compromised by 'interviewer effect' whereby respondents may regard the status of the interviewer, i.e. their social class, age, gender, ethnicity, etc. as threatening in some way. This may produce distorted data.

Interpretivist sociologists are critical of social surveys. Many surveys use fixed-response questionnaires. These may create frustration for the respondents because they may not reflect the reality of their lives. This might account for low non-response in some surveys. Also, quantitative data tells us little about people's feelings or motives.

To conclude, quantitative methods are popular but are now more likely to be used as part of a plurality of methods (triangulation). The validity of quantitative data is now likely to be strengthened by the collection of qualitative data from unstructured interviews and observation techniques.

e) **Using material from any studies with which you are familiar, assess the usefulness of participant observation.** [20 marks]

Note, the question focuses on the use of sociological studies. Item C reminds you of some of them.

e) Interpretivist sociologists believe that it is only by participating fully in the activities of the group they are studying that they can understand the subject's point of view, their cultural meanings, etc. They believe that participant observation is more useful than other methods because it is naturalistic. Behaviour is observed in its everyday setting. Experiments and social surveys, on the other hand, are artificial.

Note that the question stresses 'assess', i.e. don't forget to evaluate the method!

Trust and rapport can be established resulting in more valid data. Observation does not impose the researcher's definition of what is important on those being studied. As Bill Whyte said 'As I sat and listened, I learned answers to questions I would not have had the sense to ask if I had been getting my information solely on an interviewing basis.' Observation may uncover taken-for-granted assumptions by observing what people actually do rather than what they say they do. American police officers claimed in interviews with Cicourel that they were not racist. Observation showed otherwise. However, positivists claim that participant observation is unscientific and therefore not very useful because the presence of outsiders may bring about artificial behaviour in respondents. In Bill Whyte's study Doc started to think about how he would justify his behaviour to Whyte. Positivists claim observation lacks objectivity because many researchers 'go native'. Objectivity is also lost because of the need to be selective. What is selected depends upon the sociologist's interpretations of what is important. Observation is difficult to replicate because it is unsystematic and its results are rarely quantified. Finally, it is difficult to generalise from such studies because the samples are so small.

Today, observation tends to used in conjunction with quantitative methods as part of a triangulation approach.

Practice examination questions

Item A

You have been asked to assess a research design which is concerned with the study of the supply and use of illegal drugs in schools and colleges. You have been asked to include both state and private schools in your study. The design intends to:

- randomly select two state and two private schools in the area
- compile a quota sample of teenage males and females by asking pupils to volunteer to take part in interviews about drug use in schools
- train teachers in interviewing techniques so that they can interview pupils in class-time, using structured interviews about their knowledge and use of drugs.

Item B

Prevalence of drug trying (14–16 years)			
	Year 1	Year 2	Year 3
Ever tried	36%	47%	51%
Tried in past year	31%	41%	41%
Tried in past month	20%	26%	28%

Source: ISDD 1995

1 In your own words, briefly explain the concept of validity. [8 marks]

2 Identify and explain the main weaknesses of the research design in Item A. [35 marks]

3 In your own words, summarise the data provided in Item B concerning the prevalence of drug trying amongst 14–16 year olds. [14 marks]

4 Outline in detail and briefly assess one method which might be effective in exploring reasons for soft drug use amongst young people. [33 marks]

Chapter 2

The family

The following topics are covered in this chapter:

- Contemporary trends in family life
- The family and industrialisation
- Family relationships

2.1 Contemporary trends in family life

After studying this section you should be able to:

- outline and assess recent demographic trends in British family life relating to marriage, child-bearing, cohabitation and marital breakdown
- demonstrate knowledge and understanding of a range of concepts and definitions relating to family and household diversity
- identify key components of the relationship between the family, state and social policy

LEARNING SUMMARY

Family ideology

AQA · U1
OCR · U2533

For many years, debate about family life in the UK has been dominated by 'an ideology of familism'. It is argued, mainly by New Right and functionalist sociologists, that there is an 'ideal family' which should have the following characteristics:

> Examiners sometimes refer to this as the 'cornflake packet family'

KEY POINT

- it should be nuclear in structure (i.e. based on father, mother and children)
- it should be based on marriage rather than cohabitation
- it should be heterosexual
- males should be the breadwinners and the disciplinarians, and females should primarily be responsible for child-care/housework. There is some acknowledgement of men 'sharing' the latter.

Consequently other family types are seen as 'deviant' especially the one-parent family. This ideology can also be seen in the media, especially in advertising. It has had some influence on government social policy, especially on the taxation and social security systems.

Marriage

AQA · U1
OCR · U2533

Some members of the New Right subscribe to the view that marriage, and therefore nuclear family life is under attack and in decline.

The New Right argue that marriage is becoming less popular, as shown by the fact that marriage rates have declined in the UK. However, the majority of people in the UK marry. Many people still see marriage as a desirable objective in their lives. The number of remarriages (i.e. in which one or both partners have been divorced) has increased as a percentage of all marriages from 15% in 1971 to 40% in 1996. These people are obviously committed to the institution of marriage despite their previous negative experience(s) of it.

Robert Chester (1985) argues that we are not witnessing a mass rejection of marriage. Rather, he suggests, people are delaying marriage. In other words, people are marrying later in life, probably after a period of cohabitation, for economic reasons.

Cohabitation

AQA   U1
OCR   U2533

Cohabitation is seen by the New Right as threatening the sanctity of marriage. It is suggested that this type of arrangement is too casual and does not involve the same sort of commitment and loyalty that marriage does. Moreover, New Right thinkers believe that children born outside of marriage are a sign of moral decline. In 1992 approximately 31% of births occurred outside of marriage.

However, studies by sociologists such as Burgoyne (1982) suggest that in most cases cohabitation is a temporary phase. Most of those who cohabit eventually marry. Social attitudes tend to support marriage rather than cohabitation. Reasons for cohabitation may be pragmatic. The cost of marriage is high especially in areas hardest hit by unemployment.

Moreover about three-quarters of births outside marriage are registered by both parents. This indicates that these births are occurring within stable relationships. Fletcher (1988) argues cohabitation and births outside marriage conceal what are in fact rather conventional nuclear families based on stable relationships – even though they are not legitimised by marriage.

Cohabitation is not exclusive to heterosexual couples. Since the 1970s society has seen the emergence of lesbian and gay cohabitation, following the decriminalisation of homosexuality. Plummer (1995) notes that between 40% and 60% of gay men are cohabiting in relationships of over one-year duration.

Marital breakdown

AQA   U1
OCR   U2533

Marital breakdown is viewed by the New Right as a profound social problem with serious costs to society and individuals.

There are three types of marital breakdown:

- Divorce refers to the legal termination of a marriage. This option is not always available in some societies.

- Separation refers to the physical separation of the spouses in that they are not living under the same roof.

- Empty shell marriage refers to a husband and wife who live together, and remain legally married, but who experience no intimate or emotional relationship – e.g. remaining together for the 'sake of the children'. It is difficult to measure how many marriages are in this state.

Divorce

There has been a steady rise in the divorce rate in the UK throughout the century. In 1961, 2 married couples per 1000 were divorced in England and Wales. By 1991, this had risen to 13. Chandler (1993) argues that if present trends continue, about 40% of current marriages will end in divorce.

Explanations for the increasing divorce rate are as follows.

- Changes in legislation: Changes in divorce law have generally made it easier and cheaper to get divorced. Before 1857, divorce was rare because it was expensive and required a private Act of Parliament. Four pieces of legislation can be identified as profoundly influencing the divorce statistics.

- The 1857 Matrimonial Causes Act made divorce easier although it was still not affordable for most social groups. It also introduced the concept of 'marital crime', i.e. divorce was granted if offences such as cruelty, desertion, etc., were proved.

- The 1949 Legal Aid and Advice Act gave financial assistance to the less well-off to help with divorce costs.

> Be aware of any proposed changes to the divorce laws.

- **The 1984 Matrimonial and Family Proceedings** Act reduced the period when couples could start to petition for divorce from three years to one year.

> **KEY POINT**
>
> **The 1969 Divorce Reform Act** became law in 1971. This has been the most profound change. Marital partners now only have to demonstrate 'irretrievable breakdown of marriage' by separating for two years. 'Quickie' divorces could still be obtained by proving marital offences. A major rise in divorce followed the implementation of this act.
>
> These changes in legislation resulted in a dramatic rise in the divorce rate especially in 1971 and in 1984/85. However, legislation is not the sole cause of higher divorce rates. Legal changes reflect changing attitudes in society.

- The functionalist, **Ronald Fletcher** sees higher divorce rates as evidence that marriage is increasingly valued. Couples are no longer prepared to put up with 'empty shell' marriages. They want partners who can offer friendship, emotional fulfilment and sexual compatibility.

- In the 1960s most divorce petitions were initiated by men. However, in the 1990s 75% of divorce petitions were taken out by women. **Thornes and Collard's (1979) survey of married couples** discovered that women expect more from marriage than men and consequently tend to be less satisfied with their marriages.

- An important influence on women's attitudes has probably been the **improvement in women's employment opportunities.** In 1994 58% of the workforce was female. Women no longer have to stay unhappily married because they are financially dependent upon their husband. However, the influence of this factor should not be exaggerated. Women's average earnings are still only 75% of men's. Women's economic independence is restricted by their dominance of part-time and low-paid work.

- **Nicky Hart (1976)** argues that many women experience a 'dual burden'. They work but are still primarily responsible for the bulk of housework and child-care. Failure by men to re-distribute power in the home may lead to divorce.

Even members of the Royal Family have experienced it.

- There has been a general liberalisation of attitudes in society. Divorce no longer carries stigma. Some sociologists like **Bryan Wilson (1988)** see such change in social attitudes as due to **secularisation,** i.e. a general decline in religious practices and thinking.

- Marriage, despite its popularity, receives little support from the State. Little public money is spent keeping marriages together despite the emotional and economic costs of divorce.

> **KEY POINT**
>
> Current trends indicate that four out of ten contemporary marriages will eventually end in divorce. Monogamy, i.e. one partner for life, may eventually be replaced by 'serial monogamy', i.e. people may have a series of relationships which result in cohabitation and/or marriage. However, as Chester says, most people spend most of their lives in a family environment and also place a high value on it. **Abbott and Wallace (1990)** argue that the statistics indicate family stability, e.g. six out of ten couples who get married in the 1990s will stay together until one of them dies.

Single-parent families

AQA U1
OCR U2533

The number of one-parent families in the UK doubled from 12% of families in 1986 to 18% in 1994. Recent projections estimate that one in three families (36%) may be single-parent by the year 2016. The great majority of single-parent families are headed by women (91%).

There are a variety of reasons why single-parent families come about.

- **Divorce and/or separation**; 53% of lone mothers are divorced.

- **Death of a husband/wife/partner**; 6% of lone mothers are widowed.

- **Unplanned pregnancy** that may be the result of a casual relationship. The media tends to focus on the number of teenage pregnancies, although, only 5% of lone parents are teenagers. However, one-third of lone mothers have never been married; 80% are under thirty years of age.

> Note that the New Right's focus on teenage pregnancies is exaggerated although the UK has a worse problem than most other Western societies.

KEY POINT

New Right thinkers such as **Murray (1990)** have suggested that single parents are at the heart of a so-called **'underclass'** or **'new rabble'** that has appeared in the inner cities. This group is allegedly socialising its children into a **dependency culture** based around voluntary unemployment, claiming benefits and crime. The New Right are also concerned about the high economic costs of one-parent families in regard to welfare payments and alleged social-security fraud. This led to the setting up of the **Child Support Agency (CSA)** and the pursuit of absent fathers for maintenance.

However, New Right attitudes have been heavily criticised by feminist and critical thinkers.

- Robert Chester argues that the ideology of familism which stresses the nuclear family ideal has led to the **negative labelling of one-parent families** by social agencies such as teachers, social workers, housing departments, police and the courts.

- Labelling may result in a **self-fulfilling prophecy**, e.g. housing officers may allocate single-parent families to problem housing estates because of negative stereotypes. Consequently their children may come into contact with deviant behaviour and are more likely to be stopped by the police, etc.

- Marxists suggest that **single parents have been scapegoated** by regular moral panics about social problems which are caused by structural factors such as unemployment, racism, the decline of the inner city, etc.

- Critical sociologists point out that there is **little material incentive to become a single parent**. The social and economic situation of many one-parent families is extremely disadvantageous, e.g. 17% of those officially classed as poor are single parents.

- Single parenthood may be a **realistic strategy** in areas characterised by poverty and high unemployment. Fathers may be deemed unnecessary by some young women because they cannot provide financial support. Moreover, single parenthood may be an escape from **domestic violence**.

- **Phoenix (1993)** and **Cashmore (1985)** argue that it is often preferable for a child to live with one caring parent than with parents who are in conflict with each other and who may scapegoat the child.

- Most single mothers eventually marry or remarry. One-parent families are likely to evolve into reconstituted families.

This is an important type of family and should not be neglected in your revision.

The **reconstituted family** or **step-family** is made up of divorced or widowed people who have remarried and their children from the previous marriage or cohabitation. Such families are on the increase because of divorce, e.g. one in fifteen families are step-families; one in twelve children were living in them in 1991.

Reconstituted families, and especially children within them, are likely to have close ties with the families of previous partners. Children may be pulled in two directions and have tense relationships with their step-parents. These families may be further complicated if the parents decide to have children of their own. Family life, therefore, may be experienced quite differently to that experienced in a conventional nuclear family unit.

The diversity of family life

AQA ▶ U1
OCR ▶ U2533

> **R.N. Rapoport** and **R. Rapoport (1982)** are very critical of the New Right's insistence that there only exists one 'ideal' family type. They note that in 1994 only 20% of nuclear families contained a division of labour in which the father was the sole breadwinner and the mother was exclusively the home-maker/child-carer. The **Rapoports** argue that family life in the UK is characterised by **diversity** – there now exists a range of family types which reflect the plurality of British society.
>
> **KEY POINT**

Post-modernists suggest that family life today is characterised by diversity, variation and instability, rather than by some sort of universal and absolute idea.

- The **Rapoports** note diversity in family structure. UK family life is made up of the conventional nuclear family, cohabiting couples with children, the one-parent family and the reconstituted family. Moreover, the study **'Villains'** by **Janet Foster (1991)** of an East End London community indicated that the lives of working-class people and its younger generation in the 1980s were still dominated by the values and traditions of extended kin such as parents and grandparents who tended to live nearby. There is also evidence that some sections of the Asian (e.g. Sikhs and East African Asians), Chinese, Greek-Cypriot, Turkish and Italian communities in the UK may be more likely to live in classic extended families in which two or three generations live under the same roof.

- The **Rapoports** note that families are households but households are not necessarily families (though some will evolve into families or may have evolved out of them), e.g. **'married couple only'** households. There is also evidence that single-person households are increasing. Surveys suggest that an increasing number of young women are electing to live alone, i.e. creative singlehood.

- Diversity also exists in **patterns of kinship**. Some modern nuclear families are 'privatised' and 'relatively isolated' from kin. However, most are part of a 'modified extended family' set-up – nuclear family members still feel obliged to kin and offer emotional and material support in times of crisis. Studies also suggest that extended ties are also important to the upper class in their attempt to maintain wealth and privilege.

- Diversity can be seen in the **internal division of labour** within families. The **Rapoports** argue that most nuclear families in the UK are now **'dual-career'** families. Some women will have responsibility for the bulk of child-care and housework. Others may have negotiated a greater, perhaps even equal input from men in the domestic sphere. (The media, for example, are fond of announcing the appearance of the so-called **'New Man'**.) Others may have found husbands who are happy to reverse traditional roles and become house-husbands.

The Rapoports conclude that a fundamental change is taking place in British family life. However, Robert Chester suggests that the Rapoports have exaggerated the degree of diversity in UK society and argues that the basic features of family life have remained largely unchanged for the majority of the population since the 1950s.

Progress check

1 Identify four aspects of family life that New Right thinkers would argue are symptomatic of family decline.
2 Explain the difference between a household and a family.
3 What is 'creative singlehood'?
4 What do sociologists mean by 'serial monogamy'?
5 Why are marriage and divorce statistics regarded as unreliable?

5   The former don't include couples who are cohabitating, whilst the latter don't include separations and empty shell marriages.
4   Serial monogamy refers to consecutive marriages or cohabitation partnerships between couples.
3   This refers to economically independent women who are postponing relationships, marriage and children until their mid to late thirties and forging an alternative consumerist lifestyle.
2   A household is a group of people, e.g. a family, a group of students or a single person living under one roof. A family is a group of people who normally live together as a household and are related to each other through marriage, blood or adoption.
1   Decline in marriage rates and rise in divorce, cohabitation and one-parent families.

2.2 The family and industrialisation

After studying this section you should be able to:

- outline the relationship between industrialisation, urbanisation and family change
- outline and assess theories that debate how society and the economy shape both the structure and functions of the family

LEARNING SUMMARY

The functionalist view of the family

AQA   U1

> Functionalists such as **Talcott Parsons (1956)** suggest that the modern nuclear family has evolved to meet the needs of industrial society. Parsons argued that the most common family type in pre-industrial society was the extended family and that this extended unit was **'multifunctional'**. It was responsible for a number of functions such as production (e.g. producing food, clothing, housing for its members), education, health care and welfare.
>
> KEY POINT

Parsons argued that the industrial revolution brought about three fundamental changes in family structure and functions:

- Early industry's demand for a **geographically mobile** workforce saw the nuclear unit breaking away from the extended unit.
- **'Structural differentiation'** was also brought about by industrialisation. Specialised agencies developed which gradually took over many of the family's functions. In particular, factories took over the production function and family-members became wage earners. The State eventually took over the

functions of education, health and welfare. Parsons argued that the modern family is left with two basic and irreducible functions:

> **KEY POINT**
>
> - the **primary socialisation of children**
> - the **stabilisation of adult personality:** the married couple provide emotional support to each other to counter the stress of everyday life.

- The nuclear unit provides husband and wife with very clear **social roles**. The male is the '**instrumental leader**' and is responsible for the economic maintenance of the family group. The female is the '**expressive leader**' who is primarily responsible for socialisation of children and emotional maintenance.

In summary, then, Parsons concludes the nuclear family is **functional (beneficial) to society.** Moreover, it is beneficial for the individuals in it because it provides a stable environment for spouses and children to construct loving relationships.

Ronald Fletcher argues that the family is still heavily involved in the functions of education, health and welfare. The State has not taken over these functions. Rather, the State and the family work hand-in-hand with each other.

Wilmott and Young (1973) took issue with Parsons over the speed of change. Their empirical research conducted in a working class area (Bethnal Green) in the 1950s showed that classic extended families still existed in large numbers even at this advanced stage of industrialisation. Wilmott and Young argue that this unit only went into decline in the 1960s. There were three broad reasons for this.

- State council housing and slum clearance led to extended working-class communities being re-housed in new towns and council estates. Most new housing was geared to nuclear families.

- The Welfare State, opportunities created by the expansion of secondary education, and full employment in the 1950s undermined the need for a mutual support system.

- Consumerism became the dominant ideology in the 1960s especially as home technology, e.g. television, developed. This made the home a more attractive place.

> **KEY POINT**
>
> Wilmott and Young argued that such developments encouraged the evolution of the symmetrical family, i.e. a home-centred, privatised nuclear unit. They claimed this would become the dominant family type by the 1990s. In this sense, then, they agreed with Parsons.

This is sometimes called the 'internal critique' because these sociologists agree with Parsons that the nuclear family is the ideal type of family for industrial societies.

The historical critique of Parsons

Historians such as **Peter Laslett (1977)** and **Michael Anderson (1971)** suggest that Parsons failed to acknowledge that industrialisation may follow different patterns in different industrial societies, e.g. modern Japan still retains a commitment to the extended family form.

Laslett's survey of English parish records reveals that most **pre-industrial families were nuclear and not extended,** as Parsons claims. Laslett claims this was due to late marriage, early death and the practice of sending children away to become servants or apprentices.

Anderson's research, using data from the 1851 Census, found that the extended family was fairly common in industrial Preston. A mutual support system evolved to share scarce housing, high rents and to pool low wages.

The feminist critique of Parsons

> **KEY POINT**
>
> Marxist-feminists suggest that the **nuclear family meets the needs of capitalism** for the reproduction and maintenance of class and patriarchal inequality. It benefits the powerful at the expense of the working class and women.

The Marxist-feminist, **Margaret Benston (1972)**, argues that the nuclear family provides the basic commodity required by capitalism, i.e. labour power by:

- reproducing and rearing the future workforce at little cost to the capitalist class
- maintaining the present workforce's physical and emotional fitness through the wife's domestic labour.

She argues that capitalism essentially gets two labour powers (husband and wife) for one wage. The nuclear family acts as a stabilising force in capitalist societies because workers find it difficult to withdraw their labour power if they have families to support. **Fran Ansley (1976)** suggests that men may attempt to make up for the lack of power and control in the workplace by exerting control within the family through **domestic violence**.

> Patriarchy is an extremely important concept which is frequently focused on by examiners. Know it well! Be able to evaluate the concept.

> **KEY POINT**
>
> Radical feminists such as **Kate Millett (1970)** see modern societies and families as characterised by **patriarchy** – a system of subordination and domination in which **men exercise power over women and children**.

Millett argues that men originally acquired power over women because of biological factors (i.e. women who were frequently pregnant could not make the same contribution to society as men), but she suggests that modern technology (e.g. the pill and modern machinery) has largely rendered this legitimation of male power redundant. However, patriarchy remains in place because of ideology. Both men and women are socialised into a set of ideas which confirm male power through **gender role socialisation** as children. Moreover, this patriarchal ideology stresses the primacy of the mother-housewife role for women and the breadwinner role for men. This ensures men's domination of the labour market. Finally, Millett sees the family as legitimating violence against women.

However, some would argue that this model is dated in that it fails to consider recent trends such as the feminisation of the workforce and women's use of divorce laws. **Hakim (1995)** argues that this model fails to consider that females might be exercising rational choices in choosing domestic roles.

Progress check

1 In what way does Laslett disagree with Parsons?
2 In what ways do Anderson and Wilmott and Young disagree with Parsons?
3 What functions does the family retain according to Parsons?
4 Who benefits from the family according to Benston and Ansley?
5 What do feminist sociologists mean by 'patriarchy'?
6 Who benefits from the way families are organised, according to Millett?

6 Men.
5 Patriarchy is both a gender and an age relationship based on male authority and dominance.
4 The capitalist ruling class.
3 Primary socialisation of children and stabilisation of adult personality.
2 Parsons says it became nuclear, Anderson says it was extended. Wilmott and Young agree with Anderson but argue it became nuclear during the late 20th century.
1 Parsons says it was extended, Laslett says it was nuclear.

2.3 Family relationships

After studying this section you should be able to:

- *outline arguments relating to negative aspects of family life*
- *assess arguments relating to the changing division of labour within marriage*
- *explain the changing circumstances of both children and the elderly in British family life*

The dark side of family life

Many commentators argue that the rosy picture of nuclear family life transmitted by functionalism and the New Right obscures the contradictions that permeate family life in reality.

- If we examine criminal statistics, a very negative picture of family life emerges. Most recorded murders, assaults and child abuse – both sexual or otherwise – take place **within the family unit**. Three-quarters of all violence is domestic (and these are only the reported cases). Despite the problems in measuring the extent of **child abuse** in the UK, most experts agree that it is a major social problem today.

- **Dobash and Dobash (1992)** argue that in patriarchal societies there is still cultural support for the view that men have a 'right' to 'discipline' their wives or partners. Furthermore, there has been little institutional support offered by society to the battered wife.

- The Radical Psychiatrists, **R.D. Laing (1970) and David Cooper (1972)** argue that the family 'terrorises' children by destroying their free will, imagination and creativity. Both Laing and Cooper suggest that the family is responsible for turning imaginative children into conformist automatons.

Conjugal roles: the division of labour in marriage

Functionalist sociologists such as Parsons, Fletcher and, especially, Wilmott and Young suggest that industrialisation has led to an increase in **egalitarian marriage**, i.e. that the relationship between the spouses has become **more equal in terms of participation in housework, child-care and decision-making**.

> **Wilmott and Young** in their study *The Symmetrical Family* (1973) claimed that the extended family was characterised by **'segregated conjugal roles'**, i.e. husbands went out to work whilst wives were exclusively responsible for housework and child-care. Moreover, husbands and wives spent leisure-time apart. Wilmott and Young argued the extended family has been replaced by a privatised nuclear family characterised by **'symmetry'**. Modern marriage is characterised by **'joint conjugal roles'** meaning that women are now going out to work and men are doing a fairer share of domestic tasks. Moreover, couples were now more likely to share both leisure time and decision-making. Wilmott and Young concluded that egalitarian marriage was the norm in the symmetrical nuclear family of the 1970s.

The major challenge to the concept of symmetry has come mainly, but not exclusively, from **feminist sociologists**. Five broad areas of critique can be discerned in the sociological literature.

- **Ann Oakley (1974)** is critical of the **methodological shortcomings** of the Wilmott and Young study. She suggests that their empirical evidence is unconvincing because it was based on only one question. Moreover, their study excluded younger married women who are more likely to have young children who tend to be more time-consuming.

- A range of surveys appeared in the 1970s and 1980s which demonstrated **continuing inequalities** in the distribution of housework and child-care between husbands and wives.

> - **Elston's (1980)** survey of over 400 couples in which both partners were doctors found that 80% of female doctors reported that they took time off work to look after their sick children compared with only 2% of male doctors. Elston concluded that only a minority of professional couples in her study genuinely shared housework and child-care. Drew *et al* (1998) confirm these trends in the mid-1990s.
> - **Pahl (1984)** conducted a survey of 750 couples and discovered that unemployed men did more around the home but wives, when they were in work, were still expected to be responsible for the bulk of housework.
> - However, **Burghes (1997)** and **Beck (1992)** suggest that fathers are increasingly taking an active involvement in the emotional side of bringing up children even when marriages break down.

KEY POINT

- **Stephen Edgell (1980)** focused on the distribution of power within marriages. Edgell discovered that wives deferred to their husbands in decision-making about important issues such as buying a new house or moving job. Similarly, **Jonathan Gershuny's (1996)** survey of young married couples with children concludes that the decision to have children, although jointly reached, dramatically changes the life of the mother rather than the father – especially in regard to career advancement.

- **Barrett** argues patriarchal ideology expects women to take only jobs which are compatible with family commitments. Women are often made to feel guilty about working because they subscribe to the idea that it somehow damages their children.

- **Jesse Bernard (1976)** found the **mother–housewife role** may have negative consequences for women in terms of health.

Childhood

S. **Wagg (1992)** identifies two competing views of childhood in modern sociological literature.

- The '**Conventional**' perspective is subscribed to by child psychologists and functionalist/New Right sociologists. It views children as essentially **passive** creatures who are vulnerable to dangers such as abuse, bad parenting and sex and violence in the media. It is suggested **children need adult controls** for their own protection.

- The '**Social Construction**' perspective is influenced by **interpretivism** and is associated with the idea that childhood is a **social invention**, relative to time and place, rather than a fixed universal experience.

The interpretivist view

> **KEY POINT**
>
> **Aries (1972)** argues that childhood is not just a biological state associated with immaturity and adolescence. It is also a social experience which differs according to historical period. Historians such as Aries and **Stone (1977)** have suggested that in medieval (i.e. pre-industrial) society the idea of childhood and adolescence as separate categories to adulthood did not exist. Children were seen as 'little adults' and took part in the same work and play activities as adults. However, this idea has been challenged in recent years.

Be able to illustrate these differences with examples.

Interpretivists suggest that the experience of childhood differs according to **locality and culture**, e.g. the experience of Third World children is unlike that of British children. The experience of childhood also differs according to **social class**. There may be qualitative differences in the experience of childhood because of material differences such as poverty and wealth. The experience of childhood may differ according to **gender**. Feminists stress that the experience of gender role socialisation differs for male and female children. The experience of childhood may differ according to **ethnicity**.

> **KEY POINT**
>
> The interpretivist theory of childhood therefore suggests that there is no single universal experience of childhood. It is therefore more appropriate to talk about a **diversity of childhood experiences**. Interpretivists suggest that children are active in the construction of their own lives. It is important to understand that children interact with adults and other children and that they have some power to determine the outcome of their experience. In other words, **sociologists should attempt to see childhood through the eyes of children**.

The elderly

OCR U2583

The sociological study of the elderly is important for three reasons:

- **The numbers of the elderly are increasing**, e.g. in 1850, less than 5% of the population was aged over 65; in 1995, 15% of the population was aged over 65 and this increased to 18% in 1997 (compared with 6.5% under the age of five). Our ageing population has been caused by two factors:

Debate about the role of the elderly is on-going. Remember examiners will be impressed if you can link the sociology of old age to contemporary events and debates.

  - mortality rates have declined and life expectancy has increased due to better nutrition, higher standards of living and modern medical care
  - birth rates have declined, especially since the 1960s.

- **The elderly are not a homogeneous group.** Old age involves a wide age span (possibly 30 years) and therefore great variations in physiological and psychological functioning.

> **KEY POINT**
>
> - Like childhood, it can be argued that **the experience of old age is socially and culturally constructed** – i.e. relative to historical period, culture, locality, social class, gender, ethnicity, etc. As sociologists, we need to be aware that old age is not just a biological state – it is how the biological state is **interpreted by society** that is important.

Old age in traditional societies is regarded more positively than old age in modern industrial societies. Most old people in the UK, especially those from working class backgrounds, are **excluded from a number of areas of social life**. In particular, it is a norm to exclude people from paid work when they reach 60–65. Denial of access to work may result in isolation, loneliness, **loss of role and status** for those defined as old.

Negative stereotypes about old age based upon the association between old age, sickness and dependency are common. This is known as ageism. As Field says, old age is seen as 'a weakly stigmatised, discreditable status'. Evidence of institutional ageism may be seen in:

- Poverty – 44% of all those receiving benefits in 1997 were elderly.

- Concern expressed by governments at the rising costs of an increasing elderly population. This has led to cuts in services for old people. In recent years, the State has emphasised 'community care' for the elderly. The State intends to encourage the family to play a greater role in caring for aged parents.

If the State withdraws from the care of the elderly, there will be an increase in the number of extended families as nuclear units take on the responsibility of looking after older relatives. It is likely that this will affect the poorer sections of the community who cannot afford to invest in private care. The responsibility for the care of the elderly within the family is likely to fall to women. This may have a number of implications for females. It may further limit women's opportunities for careers and paid employment. It may reinforce patriarchal assumptions about the traditional role for females.

Progress check

1 What do sociologists mean by the 'symmetrical family'?

2 What does the word 'egalitarian' mean?

3 What is the 'dual burden' for women?

4 Identify two reasons why men might be doing more household labour than thirty years ago?

5 What do Leach, Laing and Cooper have in common?

6 Identify three influences which mean that the experience of childhood for children in the UK is not the same.

6 Social class, ethnicity and gender.
5 They are all extremely critical of family life.
4 Any from: technology has made housework less labour-intensive, more women go out to work, more men are unemployed, women are less willing to tolerate traditional male attitudes, men are under less pressure to conform to traditional ideas, etc.
3 It refers to the fact that many women go out to work yet still do the bulk of child-care and housework in the home.
2 Characterised by equality.
1 A nuclear unit in which husband and wife increasingly share child-care, housework, decision-making and leisure time.

Sample question and model answer

A typical AQA question. You will have 1 hour and 15 minutes. Spend 15 minutes reading the Items and planning your response.

Item A

According to Jon Bernardes, there are powerful lobbies in the UK which support and revere the ideal of the nuclear family. This ideal stresses a very traditional model composed of a married heterosexual couple with children. This family unit contains a sexual division of labour in which the man is the breadwinner providing economic support for his dependent wife and children. She is voluntarily housebound and happy to take care of both her husband and children's welfare.

The media often contains articles by supporters of this model complaining that women are shirking their domestic duties and damaging children by insisting on having careers. Others like John Patten, the former Secretary of State for Education, complain about the 'terrible moral and social time bomb' caused by the State backing marriage less and less and liberal laws which have allegedly resulted in dramatic increases in divorce. Consequently people are less committed to marriage and family life.

Item B

Men's participation in routine housework has increased slightly since the early 1980s but women still carry most of the burden of domestic labour, whether or not they are in waged work. Men may help more around the house, but the domestic division of labour in both Britain and the USA remains largely unaltered. Women have less free time than men and are more likely to spend it at home so that they are constantly 'on call' even when not actually working. Men have greater freedom to enjoy leisure since they do not have to consider who is taking care of the children or whether there are clean clothes ready for the next day. Someone else is doing the work and taking the responsibility.

Taken from 'Families, Households and Domestic Life' S. Jackson in S. Taylor (ed.)
Sociology: Issues and Debates, Macmillan 1999

a) What term is used by sociologists to describe the powerful lobby which supports and reveres the ideal of the nuclear family? (Item A) [2 marks]

a) New Right.

b) Identify two characteristics of the 'cornflake packet family' that people like John Patten see as ideal. [4 marks]

Note how brief these responses are. You should not over-respond to questions a–d in terms of time spent or length.

b) Any from:
- It should be nuclear in structure.
- It should be based on marriage rather than cohabitation.
- It should be heterosexual.
- Males should be the breadwinners and disciplinarians and females should primarily be responsible for childcare/housework.

c) Identify three patriarchal trends found in Item B. [6 marks]

c) Women do most of the housework whether they have a job or not.
Women have less free time than men.
Men enjoy leisure time more because they don't have to think about domestic responsibilities.

Sample question and model answer *(continued)*

d) Identify and explain two ways in which women may be resisting the trends described in Item B. [8 marks]

d) More women are indicating dissatisfaction with partners who are not willing to share child-care and housework (Thornes and Collard). This may be reflected in the fact that most divorce petitions are initiated by women.

Women may be postponing relationships, marriage and children in favour of creative singlehood. They prefer to have careers, economic independence and no responsibility, as an alternative to the dual burden described in Item B.

e) Using information from Item A and elsewhere, assess the view that liberal laws have caused dramatic rises in divorce. [20 marks]

> It is always a good idea to outline the ideas contained in the essay title before you assess.

> The question specifically asks you to use Item A.

e) In Item A John Patten from a New Right perspective argues that the State has made divorce progressively easier. His claims are partly true. The major pieces of legislation since 1945 – the 1949 Legal Aid Act and the 1969 Divorce Reform Act – were accompanied by sharp increases in the number of people seeking divorce. The latter Act introduced divorce after a period of separation on the grounds of irretrievable breakdown of marriage which made divorce a great deal easier to obtain. However, it can be argued that legal changes themselves can only come about if social attitudes have changed.

> Don't make the common mistake of assuming you have to support the argument in the essay title.

Sociologists claim there have been significant changes in social attitudes towards divorce. In particular, there is evidence that the attitude of women towards marriage and family has changed. Thornes and Collard found that women in the 1980s expected more from marriage than men and consequently tended to be less satisfied with their marriages compared with the past. These changing expectations are probably the result of economic changes in society. The increase in female employment means women are less likely to be economically dependent upon their husbands.

> Note the use of studies to challenge Patten's ideas.

Moreover, the Marxist-feminist Hart argues that working women are less likely to tolerate men not contributing to housework and child-care. Women may also object to playing a subordinate role in decision-making. All these factors may have contributed to the fact that in the 1990s women initiated the majority of divorce petitions.

There can be no doubt that there is now an increased acceptance of divorce in society. It no longer carries stigma and shame. Moreover, couples today are less willing to put up with empty shell marriages because of the effect upon children. People know they have other opportunities for happiness through remarriage. In conclusion, then, it is likely that legal changes merely reflect changes in society's attitudes.

f) With reference to Item B and other sources, assess the contribution made by feminist writers to debates about the division of labour in the family. [20 marks]

> I've started with this idea because lots of feminist research has originated in an attempt to challenge it.

f) According to Wilmott and Young's work in the 1970s, the symmetrical nuclear family is now the norm. This is characterised by egalitarian marriage and joint conjugal roles. Husband and wife are happy to share child-care, housework, decision-making and leisure time. Some empirical support for this has come from Gershuny (1992) who found that the proportion of housework performed by husbands has increased as wives have taken on paid employment.

Sample question and model answer *(continued)*

This question specifically asks you to use Item B.

It is always a good idea to address both sides of an argument as in this paragraph. This will ensure marks for evaluation.

However, not many feminist sociologists share Gershuny's optimism. A range of feminist studies have appeared in the last thirty years which demonstrate continuing inequalities in the distribution of housework and child-care between husbands and wives. Elston's survey of over 400 couples in which both partners were doctors indicated that the traditional division of labour still exerts an influence in these households. Drew et al. (1998) and Item B confirm that in the 1990s the majority of women still undertook the bulk of household tasks even when they were working. Pahl (1989) notes how men have greater power in determining how income should be spent. Also, as Jackson in Item B notes, there are domestic demands on women's leisure time that men rarely experience.

Feminist writers have been criticised for focusing on the negative side of family roles and relationships. Many people have positive experiences of family life. For example, research indicates that many women enjoy occupying traditional roles. Hakim argues women make rational choices to occupy these roles. However, feminism has made a great contribution to family sociology because it has shown how some features of family life can reflect power inequalities between men and women. It has also drawn attention to the need to get men more involved in family life and argued convincingly for changes such as maternity and paternity rights, etc. to take the strain off women. It has also raised consciousness regarding social problems such as domestic violence and therefore contributed to social change.

Practice examination questions

1   Identify and explain two key features of the reconstituted family.   [20 marks]

2   Assess the view that lone-parent families are dysfunctional.   [40 marks]

Chapter 3

Education

The following topics are covered in this chapter:

- State policy and education
- The role of education
- Explanations for differential achievement

3.1 State policy and education

After studying this section you should be able to:

- outline the relationship between state policy and the role, impact and experience of education
- assess the validity of arguments for and against comprehensive schools, selection and the marketisation of education

LEARNING SUMMARY

Social policy 1944–79

AQA   U2

> The period 1944–1979 was predominantly a social democratic era concerned with providing equal opportunities for groups such as the working class, females and ethnic minorities.
>
> **KEY POINT**

The **1944 Education Act** aimed to abolish class-based inequalities within education by making secondary education free for all – the basic principle underpinning the Act was 'equality of opportunity for all'. All children would take an IQ test at 11 (the 11+) in order to allocate them to a school suited to their abilities. The Act aimed to provide three types of secondary school (the **tripartite system**); the grammar school for the academic (20% of pupils), the secondary technical for the artistic (5%) and the secondary modern for everyone else. All schools were supposed to have similar standards of provision, i.e. 'parity of esteem'.

Criticisms of the tripartite system

Some felt that the 11+ tests were not a reliable measurement of intelligence. They were accused of being culturally biased against working-class children because of the number of working-class children disproportionately selected for the secondary moderns.

It is a good idea to have a reasonable grasp of the history of education.

Moreover, working class self-esteem was damaged by the poor image of the secondary moderns. Employers, parents and children generally viewed these schools as inferior to grammar schools. Pupils were seen as 'succeeding' to the grammar schools and 'failing' to the secondary moderns. Many middle-class children who failed the 11+ were sent into the private sector.

By the mid-1950s it was generally felt that this social policy had failed in its aims. Educational attainment was overwhelmingly class-based as most working-class children left school at 15 and entered work, whilst middle-class children continued into further and higher education.

Comprehensive schools

Be aware that questions on social policy often limit you to a historical period, e.g. 'in the past 40 years'.

> **KEY POINT**
>
> In 1965 as an attempt to apply the principle of 'equality of opportunity for all', the Labour Government abolished the tripartite system (although some Conservative councils resisted and 130 grammar schools continue to this day). The comprehensive system was introduced, based on the principle that there should be one type of school which should educate all children, regardless of social background and ability, under one roof. The general aims of such a system are to promote equal opportunities, social justice and greater tolerance for others.

Arguments in support of comprehensive education suggest that:

- Comprehensives often exist alongside both grammar schools and private schools which 'cream-off' the most able pupils. Despite this, educational standards in the form of exam results have actually improved since the 1960s according to data from the National Children's Bureau.
- High-ability children don't seem to be held back as feared. On average, they make about the same amount of progress in reading and maths as grammar school products with the same IQ.
- Lower ability children do better in comprehensives than in secondary moderns. McPherson and Williams' data suggests that the achievement of working-class children rose faster than any other social group between 1976 and 1984.

Arguments against comprehensive education suggest that:

- Class differences have largely remained unchanged. Heath (1982) concludes that comprehensive reorganisation has had little effect on the social-class inequalities that existed before 1965. Exam results have got better but the gap between top and bottom has more or less stayed the same. However, is it fair to expect schools to compensate for inequalities which are caused by the organisation of society?
- Many comprehensives stream their pupils. Evidence indicates that streaming results in social-class segregation. Working-class pupils are disproportionately found in lower streams and thus may be labelled as failures. Streaming is criticised as a form of social selection – the tripartite system under one roof.
- Comprehensives have recruited on the basis of catchment areas. This has often led to intakes being 'single-class' rather than socially mixed. Schools in more affluent areas with mainly middle-class intakes have tended to do better than schools in depressed inner-city areas with largely working-class intakes. Adonis and Pollard call this 'selection by mortgage'.
- Inner-city comprehensives have attracted a great deal of negative publicity for declining standards in terms of exam league-table positions, truancy, failed inspections, discipline problems, large class sizes, etc.

Educational social policy 1979–97

AQA   U2

> **KEY POINT**
>
> The period 1979–97 was mainly concerned with linking education to the demands of the free-market economy. Aspects of the education system such as the curriculum, qualifications and teaching were re-organised in an attempt to raise standards and produce a more flexible workforce.

Economic recession and rising unemployment, especially amongst youth, led to a fundamental change in educational social policy in the 1970s. Some politicians, especially the Labour Prime Minister, James Callaghan, and Margaret Thatcher (who became Prime Minister in 1979), suggested that poor education was a major cause of Britain's industrial decline. During 1979–97 Conservative Governments made radical changes to the organisation of schooling in order to fulfil three aims.

- To make schooling **more relevant to work** and thereby produce the skills required by industry to make Britain more competitive in the global market-place.

  The New Right claimed that the British workforce lacked technical skills needed by industry. A number of training and education schemes were developed which became collectively known as the **'new vocationalism'**. These aimed to make young people more employable by giving them work experience. These included school-based courses such as:

  - the Technical and Vocational Educational Initiative (TVEI) set up in 1980
  - the Certificate for Pre-Vocational Education (CPVE) first taught in 1985
  - General National Vocational Qualifications (GNVQ) and National Vocational Qualifications (NVQ).

  Moreover, the Youth Training Scheme (YTS) also expanded in the 1980s. After 1987, young people could be denied benefit if they refused to take part in this scheme.

- To take **more centralised control** of the curriculum and teaching methods in order to raise standards and increase efficiency.

  The **1988 Education Reform Act** was the most important piece of educational policy since 1944 and focused on more centralised state regulation of education in six ways:

  - A **national curriculum** was introduced based around three core, and seven foundation, subjects for pupils aged 5 to 16. This policy shifted power over teaching and content from teachers and examination boards to the government.

  - National **tests** at 7, 11 and 14 were introduced. The results of these (along with other criteria such as GCSE, A Level and truancy statistics) are published annually as part of **league tables** that aim to compare the performance of schools.

  - Responsibility for managing school budgets was largely removed from local authority control and given to head teachers. This was known as **'local management of schools'** (LMS).

  - Comprehensive schools were allowed to opt out and become grant-maintained schools (GM schools) on the basis of a majority parental vote. The head teachers of such schools were given complete control over the school budget and how their schools were organised and run.

  - **City Technology Colleges** (CTCs), specialising in the arts, maths, science and technology, were set up in inner-city areas. These were independent of local authorities and supposed to be financed by private industry.

  - A new system of school and college inspection was introduced.

- To **introduce** what **Burgess and Parker (1999)** call 'an atmosphere of "incentive" and "enterprise"' in schools and colleges. Policies therefore aimed to create greater diversity in education by providing a wider choice for parents.

  - Conservative governments encouraged diversity through **specialisation** – e.g. by 1996 there were 15 CTCs and over 180 language or technology colleges.

- **Selection** was encouraged in a number of ways. The 130 grammar schools continued undisturbed alongside the comprehensive system. GM schools were allowed to introduce parental interviews and tests in order to select their intakes.

- Parents were given the right to send their children to the school of their choice – 'open enrolment'. Schools now had to compete for students and league tables and school prospectuses were published to assist parental choice.

- Private education was encouraged. The **Assisted Places Scheme** provided bright children from less advantaged backgrounds in state schools with free places in private schools.

New Labour educational policy – 1997 onwards

AQA ▷ U2

In 1997 New Labour were elected and, generally speaking, their educational policy retains the New Right emphasis on selection, standards, choice and diversity. For example:

- Grant-maintained schools have been re-named '**foundation schools**'. They no longer receive grants from central government but they still retain special status and therefore have a great deal of autonomy in how they recruit and select pupils.

- Grammar schools continue to exist. It was announced in March 2000 that New Labour had no intention of abolishing them.

- The **Assisted Places Scheme** has been abolished but Labour has no plans to abolish or reform private education.

You should keep a record of any significant changes to education made by New Labour.

- There are plans to apply tighter control over quality and standards. Some schools will be publicly identified as underachieving ('**naming and shaming**') in regard to poor exam results, high rates of truancy and exclusion and discipline problems.

> However, New Labour's educational policy is distinctive in some respects from the previous government – leading some commentators to describe it as a '**third way**'. In particular, a renewed emphasis on **improving the opportunities of disadvantaged groups** is demonstrated by the following:

KEY POINT

- The **New Deal** aims to improve educational opportunities for the long-term unemployed and single mothers by giving them financial assistance to attend further education.

- Labour's educational policy is based on the concept of '**social inclusion**', which argues that education, especially at the further and higher levels, has traditionally excluded certain groups, e.g. the unemployed, single mothers, the elderly, etc. The current idea is that choice and diversity in education should be accessible to all social groups – i.e. '**widening social participation**'.

- **Excellence in Cities** – this £350-million programme has led to the creation of '**education action zones**' in six major cities in which extra help will be given to underachievers in schools.

Progress check

1 Identify two academic costs associated with comprehensive education.

2 Identify two social costs associated with selection.

3 What was the Assisted Places Scheme?

4 What type of schools were underpinned by equality of opportunity?

5 Suggest two ways in which the local administration of schools has been weakened since 1970.

6 Briefly define what is meant by a 'grant-maintained school'.

1 It is argued that 'clever' children are held back or not fully stretched. Large classes may mean individuals don't get special attention in terms of needs and talents.
2 Middle-class pupils and parents are 'creamed off' from the state sector. It may reinforce social divisions.
3 Introduced in 1980 to assist less affluent parents with the costs of sending their children to certain private schools.
4 Comprehensive schools.
5 The 1988 Educational Reform Act introduced a national curriculum and testing at 7, 11 and 14.
6 Until 1998 schools could opt out of local authority control. Such schools received an 'enhanced' direct grant from central government rather than being funded through the LEA.

3.2 The role of education

After studying this section you should be able to:

- identify different explanations of the role of education
- define and illustrate the concept of 'the hidden curriculum'
- describe the relationship between education, training and the economy
- explain the concept of 'meritocracy'

Functions of education

 AQA U2

It can be argued that education has three broad functions as described below.

Socialising young people into key cultural values.

This process is often referred to as cultural or social reproduction.

> **KEY POINT**
>
> Functionalists such as Durkheim and Parsons saw education as an essential agency of socialisation whose function is to transmit common values to the next generation – a process crucial to the maintenance of social order in society.

Parsons argued that schools act as a bridge between the family and wider society, with the role of education being to promote universal values such as achievement, individualism, competition and equality of opportunity. Durkheim argued that the teaching of subjects like English, history and religious education is central to social solidarity because it enables children to feel a sense of belonging to society.

> **KEY POINT**
>
> Marxists such as Louis Althusser, argue that education is an ideological state apparatus whose main function is to maintain, legitimate and reproduce (generation by generation) class inequalities in wealth and power.

The role of education is ideological – it promotes capitalist values as common values. Althusser argued this is mainly done through the **hidden curriculum** – the informal ways in which conformity, and acceptance of failure and inequality are encouraged in working-class young people.

Althusser identified two ways in which the hidden curriculum convinces the working class that the capitalist system is fair and natural.

Why might sociology be excluded?

- **Through the knowledge which is taught in schools**: students rarely come into contact with ways of thinking that are critical and which challenge inequality. Marxist thinkers have criticised the national curriculum as 'highly prescriptive' and suggest that subjects such as economics, politics and sociology have been deliberately excluded for ideological reasons.

- **The way that schools are organised**: the everyday rules and routines of schools transmit very different messages to middle-class and working-class pupils about the purpose of school. Devices such as streaming and examinations serve to convince working-class pupils that their knowledge and experiences are irrelevant and to accept failure as their fault.

Marxists see education as producing a conformist labour force which passively accepts its lot.

Teaching the skills required by a developing economy

Questions which use the term 'training' often require an evaluation of the new vocationalism.

Functionalists claim that there is a strong relationship between education and the economy. As the economy becomes more complex, it requires new skills and greater technical expertise, and education must provide a labour force to meet these needs. However, New Right politicians in the late 1970s were convinced that education had failed to fulfil this role convincingly. In response to these fears, the Conservative Government developed the 'new vocationalism'.

Marxists, in criticism, claim that education is not about transmitting skills, but about transmitting 'good worker' attitudes. **Bowles and Gintis** argue that capitalism requires a docile workforce prepared to accept low skills and pay. They, too, focus on the hidden curriculum of schools.

> Bowles and Gintis note that what goes on in schools 'corresponds' with what goes on in factories. Most work is boring and routine (e.g. assembly-line production in factories) and school functions to prepare working-class pupils for their future role as factory workers, e.g. they note that students are socialised into accepting authority, powerlessness, different rewards for different abilities and lack of satisfaction.

KEY POINT

Marxists are particularly critical of the new vocationalism and especially YTS.

- Phil **Cohen** argued that the real function of YTS was to cultivate in young people conformist attitudes, work discipline and the acceptance of a future of low-paid and unskilled work with frequent bouts of unemployment and job changes.

- Andy **Green's** research indicated that most schemes resulted in trainees getting low paid jobs which were relatively unskilled and insecure.

- Vocational schemes help to legitimise class divisions because they encourage the idea that the working class are trained whilst the middle class are educated. In this sense, they are another form of selection.

Allocating people to the most appropriate job

Selection is increasingly a focus of exam questions.

> **KEY POINT**
>
> The functionalists **Davis and Moore** argue that the role of education is to allocate people to occupations which best suit their abilities. Educational mechanisms such as grades, examinations, references and qualifications are used to sort individuals. Society is thus a meritocracy in which people are rewarded for intelligence, ability and effort.

Moreover, both the most talented and the least talented will end up in jobs in which they will make efficient contributions to the smooth running of capitalist society. In this sense, inequality is functional and necessary.

Marxists and other critical thinkers reject the view that the UK educational system is meritocratic for three broad reasons:

- They argue that as long as private education continues to exist society can never be meritocratic, because public schools symbolise class inequality. However, supporters of private education believe it to be an essential part of a free market.

- Some argue that the focus on choice has created a hierarchy of educational institutions based on forms of **selection** rather than equal opportunities. In the secondary sector, both grammar schools and foundation schools practise overt selection whilst 'selection by mortgage' is becoming a norm in the comprehensive sector. The focus on parental choice and league tables has created an incentive for schools to be more selective in their intake and exclude children likely to perform badly.

  As money and resources follow pupils, schools in deprived inner-city areas find it difficult to attract pupils and resources. They consequently 'sink' to the bottom of league tables, which undermines staff and pupil morale and makes it difficult to escape from the spiral of failure and potential closure.

- The concept of meritocracy is undermined by the disproportionate inequalities in achievement experienced by groups such as the working class and particular ethnic minorities in the British education system.

Similarities in the Functionalist and Marxist approaches to education

AQA   U2

You should be aware that, despite their differences, functionalist and Marxist accounts of education do share three broad similarities.

Many students know the differences, but in a 'compare and contrast' question it is important to know the similarities.

> **KEY POINT**
>
> - they are both **structuralist** theories in that they see social institutions as more important than individuals.
> - they do not pay much attention to **classroom interaction** or how both teachers and pupils interpret what goes on in schools.
> - Paul Willis provides a major critique of both perspectives by pointing out that both theories are **over-deterministic**, i.e. both see pupils as passive products of the educational system. Functionalists see pupils being turned into model citizens whilst Marxists argue that working-class kids are turned into conformist workers. Both theories fail to take into account the **power of pupils to resist** these processes. In Willis' study, 'Learning to Labour', the lads took little notice of the hidden curriculum – they substituted their own definitions of what school was about, based upon 'having a laff'. The lads in his study were quite happy to take factory jobs because their working-class culture valued factory work. Taking such jobs was seen as success rather than failure.

Progress check

1 Identify two ways in which schools act as agents of socialisation.

2 What is the 'new vocationalism'?

3 What do sociologists mean by the term 'cultural reproduction'?

4 Suggest two reasons why achievement is often measured through certification?

5 Define the concept 'hidden curriculum'.

6 What do functionalist sociologists mean when they describe education as meritocratic?

6 They believe that intelligence, effort and achievement are the main criteria for educational mobility and rewards.

5 This refers to the way in which cultural values and attitudes (e.g. obedience to authority, conformity, etc.) are transmitted through teaching and the organisation of schools.

4 Any of the following: Certificates are indicative of the time spent in formal education. They are seen as indicating personal worth/status. They are seen as objective indicators or measurements of ability and/or achievement/performance. They have a job-market value. They help to measure quality of education, e.g. school league tables.

3 The socialisation of each generation into the cultural values of society (functionalism) or the ruling class (Marxism).

2 Work-experience oriented courses introduced into schools in the 1980s, e.g. TVEI, CPVE, NVQ, etc. and Youth Training.

1 Any two of the following: They socialise pupils into key social values such as achievement, competition and individualism. They encourage social integration through the teaching of English, History and RE. They transmit key skills. They encourage conformity through the hidden curriculum.

3.3 Explanations for differential achievement

After studying this section you should be able to:

- outline and assess different explanations of the relationship between achievement, social class, ethnicity and gender
- identify relationships and processes occurring within schools that impact on achievement, including teacher–pupil relationships, pupil subcultures and the organisation of teaching and learning

LEARNING SUMMARY

Class and achievement

At all stages of education, students from working-class backgrounds achieve less than their middle-class counterparts. Even when the former have the same level of intelligence as the latter, they:

- are less likely to be found in nursery schools or pre-school playgroups
- are more likely to start school unable to read
- are more likely to fall behind in reading, writing and maths skills
- are more likely to be placed in lower sets or streams
- are more likely to get fewer GCSEs or low grades
- are more likely to leave school at the age of 16
- are less likely to go on into the sixth form and on to university.

Ethnicity and achievement

Children from Indian backgrounds do as well as, and often better than, white children. However, children from Pakistani/Bangladeshi homes and males from Afro-Caribbean (West Indian) homes tend to get fewer and poorer GCSE results than white or Indian children. They are less likely to get A Levels and go on to university. West Indian males are over-represented in special schools for children with behavioural or learning difficulties. However, not all Pakistani/Bangladeshi and West Indian pupils do badly. Those who come from middle-class backgrounds achieve greater academic success than those who come from working-class backgrounds. Also, females generally achieve greater academic success than males from the same background.

There are essentially four broad explanations of educational underachievement which can be applied to social class and racial inequalities in education.

Intelligence

Some New Right sociologists argue that working-class and black people have lesser innate intelligence as shown by IQ tests. However, it is impossible to separate genetic influences from environmental influences such as poverty, education, racism, etc. which may exert greater influence. IQ tests may be culture-biased and can never be neutral because they measure what middle-class academics regard as intelligence. Performance in them may simply measure length of time spent in education.

Cultural deprivation theory

> This blames working-class culture and ethnic-minority culture for failure to achieve. It suggests that the reason working-class and ethnic-minority children fail is because their home culture is inadequate, especially in terms of parental attitudes, child-rearing practices and language development.
>
> **KEY POINT**

- **JWB Douglas** argues that working-class and ethnic-minority parents are less interested in their children's education. He measured parental interest by counting the number of times parents visited schools for parents' evenings, etc.

- The **Newsons** argued middle-class, white parents are more child-centred than working-class and ethnic-minority parents.

- **Bernstein** suggested working-class and ethnic-minority children suffer from linguistic deprivation.

- **Cultural Deprivation** theory influenced educational policy in the 1960s and led to the founding of six Educational Priority Areas. These were deprived inner-city areas and extra money was spent on their primary schools. This type of scheme was known as **positive discrimination** or **compensatory education** because it aimed to discriminate positively in favour of the working class and compensate for 'deficiencies' in working-class culture.

Criticisms of cultural deprivative theory include the following:

- It is methodologically suspect – is counting the number of times a parent visits a school a reliable indicator of parental interest? It is also ethnocentric – it dismisses working-class culture as irrelevant.

- It fails to take account of **material deprivation**. Factors such as poverty may be more important than attitudes in explaining the failure of working-class and ethnic-minority children to stay on in post-16 education. These groups may have less access to material resources such as educational toys and games, private playgroups and nurseries, etc. They may be trapped in a cycle of poverty. Ethnic minorities might be denied access to jobs and decent housing because of racism.

Be able to illustrate Bernstein's ideas with reference to elaborate and restricted language codes.

The Marxist view

Be able to distinguish between economic capital (i.e. wealth) and cultural capital (i.e. linguistic and cultural competencies).

The Marxist, Bourdieu, points out that schools are middle-class institutions, run by the middle-class for the middle-class. Working-class and ethnic-minority children may lack the cultural capital required (i.e. middle-class values) for academic success in these institutions. Education functions to ensure that the working class and ethnic minorities accept their position at the bottom of society. These groups are doomed to failure because their success would threaten the ruling-class monopoly of wealth and power.

Labelling theory

AQA   U2
OCR   U2533

Labelling theory provides the fourth broad explanation of underachievement. This theory focuses exclusively on **school factors** and specifically **classroom interaction between teachers and pupils.**

- It argues that teachers judge or **label** pupils on the basis of factors such as social class, gender, race, behaviour, attitude, appearance, etc. rather than ability and intelligence. Middle-class white pupils are seen as 'ideal pupils' and therefore receive more positive teacher attention than working-class and ethnic-minority pupils. Studies such as **Becker and Rist** confirm that ideal pupils tend to be pupils who have conformed to the demands of the hidden curriculum.

Be able to identify at least two criticisms of the self-fulfilling prophecy theory.

- According to **Rosenthal and Jacobsen**, teachers somehow communicate these labels to pupils and eventually the pupils internalise them. Interaction with teachers on the basis of labels may result in a **self-fulfilling prophecy.**

- Positive labelling may lead to white middle-class pupils being streamed more highly than working-class and ethnic-minority pupils. **Streaming** is a form of institutional labelling. **Keddie** discovered that top streams are treated more favourably than bottom streams in terms of teacher control and access to high-status knowledge, while bottom-stream pupils pick up the hidden-curriculum message that failure is their fault.

- Pupils with a negative self-image as a result of labelling may turn to **deviant sub-cultures** to compensate for lack of status from teachers. **Hargreaves** notes that pupils award each other the status denied to them by the school by carrying out anti-school behaviour. This confirms their failure in the school's eyes.

Criticism of this theory are as follows:

- It ignores social influences external to the classroom, e.g. Marxists point out that schools are shaped by social-class inequalities rooted in the organisation of wider capitalist society.

- **Willis** argues that this theory underestimates working-class culture. Boys don't fail because they are labelled by teachers. Many of them reject qualifications because they don't see them as relevant to the type of factory jobs they want to do. Their behaviour is a result of a conscious choice to reject schooling rather than a reaction to teacher labelling (which they resist).

- Other studies, e.g. **Fuller**, note that pupils can **resist** teacher labels. A negative label may result in hard work to disprove the label.

- There is little empirical evidence in support of the a self-fulfilling prophecy.

Gender and achievement

AQA   U2
OCR   U2533

> Until the late 1980s, the major concern was with the underachievement of girls. They were less likely than boys to pursue A Levels or enter higher education. However, in the early 1990s, girls had begun to outperform boys at most levels of the education system. The main focus today therefore is on the underachievement of boys. However, there are still concerns about the subject choices made by girls, e.g. they are still less likely than boys to apply for degree courses in the hard sciences and information technology. This may impact on post-educational opportunities in terms of training and jobs.

Why are girls now succeeding?

There is some evidence that the women's movement has raised female expectations. Many women are looking beyond the mother–housewife role as illustrated by Sue Sharpe, who in a 1976 survey, discovered that girls' priorities were 'love, marriage, husbands, children, jobs and careers, more or less in that order'. When the research was repeated in 1994, she found that the priorities had changed to 'job, career and being able to support themselves'.

There are increasing job opportunities for women in the service sector of the economy. Many girls have mothers in paid employment who provide positive role models for them. Females now recognise that the future offers girls more choices – economic independence and careers are a real possibility.

E.g. girls into Science and Technology (GIST).

The work of feminist sociologists in the 1980s, especially Dale Spender, Michelle Stanworth and Alison Kelly, highlighted the educational underperformance of girls and led to a greater emphasis on equal opportunities in schools. Policies included monitoring teaching and teaching materials for sex bias to ensure more girl-friendly schooling, especially in the sciences. Teachers are now more sensitive about avoiding gender stereotyping in the classroom.

There is mounting evidence that girls work harder, are more conscientious and are better motivated than boys. Girls put more effort into their work and spend more time on coursework and homework. They take more care with presentation, are better organised and consequently meet deadlines better than boys do.

Changes in the organisation of education may have benefited girls – the national curriculum's emphasis on science means that girls cannot avoid doing some hard science.

Why are boys underachieving?

Teachers' gender-biased expectations of male and female behaviour may result in them not being as strict with boys as with girls, i.e. they expect boy's work to be late, to be untidy and boys to be disruptive.

Browne and Mitsos (1998) suggest boys lose valuable learning time by messing about, getting sent out of the room and by being excluded. Four out of every five permanent exclusions from school are boys.

This issue is constantly in the news – make a note of any research you see reported in the papers.

The major decline in traditional male jobs may have influenced boys' motivation and ambition, i.e. they may feel that qualifications are a waste of time because there are only limited job opportunities. This may even involve constructing alternative self-esteem and status systems around delinquent or anti-school activities.

Some commentators, notably **Mac En Ghaill**, suggest that boys are experiencing a **'crisis of masculinity'** which means that they feel unsure about their role in the light of these economic changes. The future looks bleak and without purpose so they don't see the point in working hard.

Boys appear to gain **'street cred'** and peer group status for not working. Some researchers (e.g. Willis) have discovered that anti-education and anti-learning subcultures exist in some schools. Schoolwork is seen as 'uncool' and in particular, reading is regarded as boring, 'sissy', feminine and to be avoided at all costs. This may explain why boys lack the application for coursework skills.

> Go beyond gender!

This debate is also influenced by **social class and gender**. Although working-class and middle-class girls do better than working-class and middle-class boys, respectively, middle-class boys out-perform working-class girls. Moreover, girls from some ethnic backgrounds also perform significantly worse than middle-class boys. The explanations for the under-achievement of working-class and some ethnic-minority girls may have more to do with traditional social class-based explanations (e.g. cultural and material deprivation, etc.) than explanations which are unique to gender.

Progress check

1 What theory of achievement is described by the phrase 'what teachers believe, their students will achieve'?

2 Identify two ways in which the concept of the self-fulfilling prophecy has been criticised.

3 Explain what Marxist sociologists mean by cultural capital.

4 Identify two home or family factors which allegedly hold back some working-class pupils according to cultural deprivation theory.

5 What is meant by material deprivation?

6 Who said that schools are middle-class institutions run by the middle class for the middle class?

6 Bourdieu.

5 Deprivation that is caused by lack of economic opportunity; e.g. poverty.

4 Parental attitudes, poor child-rearing practices, inferior language codes, etc.

3 Bourdieu is referring to the cultural advantages that middle-class parents can endow their children with for success in the middle-class educational system, e.g. linguistic and cultural competencies.

2 There is little empirical evidence for it. Pupils may resist such processes.

1 Labelling theory.

Sample question and model answer

A typical AQA question. You will have 1 hour and 15 minutes. Spend 15 minutes reading the data and planning your response.

Item A

About one in ten people become hostile to school according to a survey carried out by the National Commission on Education published in 1993. The survey sampled more than 2000 young people aged to 11 to 13 years and found that lessons became less interesting for pupils as they progressed from 11 to 13 years of age. By the age of 13, one in five said they often counted the minutes to the end of a lesson and one in ten reported that they were bored in all or most lessons. Only 60% of the 13 year old sample reported that they were happy at school. Truancy was common in the early years of secondary school; 9% of 11 year olds admitted that they had 'bunked off' school during the year, a figure which rose sharply to 32% for the 13 year olds. Such trends are particularly worrying for schools because truancy figures have to be published as part of their league tables.

(Adapted from M. Denscombe, Sociology Update, *Olympus Books, 1994)*

1 hour should be spent writing.

Item B

A process of stratification occurs in many classrooms with teachers meting out different treatment to more- or less-favoured groups of pupils. Green (1985) analysed interaction between teachers and pupils in three junior and three middle schools. This study concluded that boys of European origin were particularly favoured by teachers whilst girls and boys of Afro-Caribbean origin received much less individual attention and considerably less praise and encouragement. However, such accounts can be criticised as over-deterministic. Other studies have focused on the efforts of pupils to actively create their own identities and perhaps even adopt resistance strategies to teacher labelling.

(Adapted from P. Bilton et al., Introductory Sociology, *3rd Edition, Macmillan, 1996)*

Don't over-respond to questions a–d in terms of time spent and length.

a) What do you think sociologists mean by the term 'over-deterministic'? (Item B) [2 marks]

a) The phrase 'over-deterministic' is generally used as a criticism of sociological theories which imply that people have no choice but to behave in the way they do because of social factors beyond their control. The criticism suggests that people can resist these processes.

b) Identify two strategies a school can adopt to minimise truancy and therefore improve its league tables. (Item A) [4 marks]

b) There are seven possible answers to this question:
- By making lessons more interesting for pupils.
- By not admitting 'problem' pupils.
- By introducing a selection policy, such as interviewing prospective pupils and parents.
- By improving the quality of teaching and/or resources.
- By not entering some people for exams.
- By redefining absence.
- By addressing and attempting to solve the problem of truancy.

Sample question and model answer *(continued)*

c) Identify and briefly explain three possible sociological explanations for truancy. (Item A) **[6 marks]**

c) Possibilities include:
- Some children from economically deprived backgrounds may truant because their poverty may create embarrassment in terms of incomplete uniform, free school dinners, etc.
- Some children may be experiencing a form of cultural deprivation. They may not attend school because of a lack of parental or community control due to education not being valued.
- Some pupils may believe that unrealistic academic expectations have been put on them by parents and/or teachers.
- Truanting with peers may be more attractive in terms of status and excitement than attendance at school.
- Truancy may be a reaction to being negatively labelled by teachers.
- Some kids may not be able to identify with what goes on in schools.

d) With reference to Item B and other sociological evidence, assess the view that ethnic minority pupils are discriminated against in the education system. **[20 marks]**

You have specifically been asked to use Item B. Remember, if you do not, you are throwing potential marks away.

d) Item B notes that the labelling theory has played a major role in suggesting that ethnic minorities are discriminated against in the education system. Interactionists have argued that teachers see white pupils as ideal pupils, and negatively label Afro-Caribbean pupils' behaviour. Brittan found that teachers saw black pupils as less able, disruptive and lazy. Wright's study concluded that such stereotyping led to interaction between white teachers and black students being characterised by conflict and confrontation. In Item B, Green suggests that Afro-Caribbean children receive less attention, praise and encouragement from teachers.

Such labelling may lead to problems. First, ethnic minority pupils may be placed in lower bands on the basis of stereotypes rather than ability. Green notes that labelling has a negative effect upon self-esteem and may result in a self-fulfilling prophecy as black children give up. Deviant and racially exclusive anti-school cultures may develop which award status on the basis of delinquent activities.

Here's the assessment as demanded.

As Item B points out, labelling theory has been criticised for being over-deterministic. It does seem to give those labelled little choice over their future. There is evidence that some ethnic-minority pupils have resisted teacher labelling. For example, Fuller's study of a group of black girls in a North London comprehensive school found that the girls resented being labelled negatively for being female and black. They therefore set out to prove teachers wrong and devoted themselves to hard work.

Labelling theory is also criticised because it neglects home and cultural factors such as parental lack of interest and language problems. Other critical sociologists, however, blame poverty and racism. Labelling theory also tends to underplay social class. Middle-class ethnic minorities tend to do a lot better than those of working-class origin. The situation is further complicated by the fact that some ethnic minority groups, especially Indian females and Chinese, achieve excellent results.

Sample question and model answer (continued)

Note the question focuses on social class, not gender or ethnicity.

e) Using material from the Items and elsewhere, assess the extent to which classroom practices can influence the achievement of working-class pupils.

[20 marks]

Labelling theory focuses on how classroom practices may cause working-class underachievement. Becker argues that teachers operate in the classroom with stereotypes of what constitutes an 'ideal pupil'. Teachers judge and label pupils on the basis of their social class, gender, race, family background, dress and behaviour. Intelligence and ability, says Becker, are secondary influences. Working-class backgrounds may be judged negatively compared with middle-class backgrounds. Becker notes that labels are communicated to children via interaction with the teacher. Becker and Rosenthal and Jacobsen point out that pupils may internalise negative teacher labels and consequently under-achieve. This is known as a self-fulfilling prophecy. Teacher expectations are also institutionalised through streaming. Those in the bottom streams may pick up negative messages about their ability from teachers and fail or set up anti-school deviant sub-cultures which confirm teacher predictions. Working-class children are disproportionately found in bottom streams. As Item A implies, truancy may also be a response to this.

Note how classroom practices are quickly linked to a specific sociology theory.

Here's the assessment.

Labelling theory has been criticised for over-emphasising classroom practices. Bourdieu argues that the hidden curriculum of schools ensures working-class failure because schools are middle-class institutions run by the middle class in order to ensure middle class success. Pupils from working-class backgrounds therefore are deliberately deprived of the cultural capital required for success in education.

Labelling theory has also been criticised for being over-deterministic. Willis, however, rejects the idea that teacher labelling has any influence. His study of working-class lads indicated that they actually wanted working-class jobs because that was the norm in their families and community. They therefore took little notice of how teachers labelled them.

Finally, cultural deprivationists argue that working-class failure is located in the home environment and specifically the lack of parental interest in children's education, the deficiency of child-rearing practices and linguistic deprivation. Truancy therefore may be quite simply a reflection of working-class culture failing to value education. However, Halsey argues that working-class failure at school and truancy may be caused by material factors such as poverty.

Practice examination questions

1 Identify and explain two sub-cultural responses to or labelling by teachers.

[10 marks]

2 Outline and assess the view that female underachievement in schools is a thing of the past.

[40 marks]

Chapter 4

The individual and society

The following topics are covered in this chapter:

- Introducing the individual and society
- Culture and the formation of identity

4.1 Introducing the individual and society

After studying this section you should be able to:

- outline the role of values, norms and the agents of socialisation in the formation of culture
- explain how social roles are learned and how expected patterns of behaviour regulate social life

LEARNING SUMMARY

Culture and identity

OCR | U2532

Culture is generally defined as the way of life of a society – what **Kluckhohn** calls a 'design for living'. **Marshall (1998)** suggests that 'in social science, culture is socially rather than biologically transmitted'. By culture, he means the shared values, norms and beliefs of a society as well as the shared meanings and symbols (such as language) which people use to make sense of their world.

Know your concepts well.

> **Values** are defined as widely accepted beliefs that something is worthwhile and desirable, e.g. a high value is placed on human life. **Norms** are essentially values put into practice – specific rules of behaviour relative to specific social situations. For example, people generally wear black at funerals in the UK. Turning up in a pink tuxedo would be regarded as norm-breaking behaviour, i.e. as **deviant**. There are norms governing all aspects of human behaviour from going to the toilet to boiling an egg.
>
> **KEY POINT**

All members of society are accorded a social position by culture, i.e. **statuses**. Generally sociologists distinguish between **ascribed statuses** and **achieved statuses**. The former are fixed at birth usually by inheritance or biology – gender and race are fixed characteristics which result in women and ethnic minorities occupying low-status roles in some societies. However, status in this respect is the result of the dominant culture, e.g. male and white, defining these characteristics as inferior. Achieved statuses are statuses over which individuals have control – in Western societies, status is achieved through education, jobs and even marriage.

Society expects those of a certain status to behave in particular ways. A set of norms is imposed on a status, collectively known as a role. For example, doctors are expected by patients to maintain confidentiality and to behave professionally.

Sociobiologists argue that human behaviour is largely the product of nature. However, sociologists generally agree that human behaviour is not instinctive. If human behaviour is influenced by biology at all, it is only at the level of physiological need, i.e. we must sleep, eat, defecate, etc. However, even these **biological influences are shaped by culture**. For example, cultural values and norms usually determine what is eaten (e.g. insects are not popular foodstuffs in the UK) and how we eat (e.g. table manners).

Human cultures are enormously diverse. Values, norms, statuses and roles differ from society to society. This can lead to cultural stereotyping because what is a normal type of behaviour may be seen as deviant or extreme in another. For example, Islamic societies are often labelled and judged by the West as 'fanatical'. Sociologists believe that it is important not to see culture as absolute, fixed and universal. Rather, they argue in favour of **cultural relativity** – meaning no one culture is superior or inferior. They are merely different.

Socialisation

OCR ▸ U2532

Societies operate effectively because members of society learn culture – which needs to be transmitted generation by generation to ensure that it is shared. Shared culture allows society's members to communicate and co-operate. The process of learning culture is known as socialisation – a process that involves internalising the norms and values of a culture so that ways of thinking, behaving and seeing things are taken for granted.

> The family, specifically parents, are central to **primary socialisation** which is the first stage in a lifelong process. Children learn language and basic norms and values. These can be taught formally but they are more likely to be picked up informally by **imitating parents**. Parents may use **sanctions** to reinforce approved behaviour and punish unacceptable behaviour. Such processes help children learn about their role in the family and in society.

KEY POINT

A range of other institutions participate in the socialisation of children – these are **secondary agents of socialisation**. For example, schools, religion and the mass media all play a role in teaching society's members how to behave in particular formal contexts.

Fulcher and Scott's book is *Sociology*, OUP (1999), p.124.

> Socialisation in all its varied forms involves children interacting with others and becoming aware of themselves as individuals. 'Children come to see themselves as conscious and reflective entities – agents or subjects – capable of independent and autonomous action'. (Fulcher and Scott, 1999). Socialisation is the process through which **children acquire identities**.

KEY POINT

Identity

OCR ▸ U2532

Be able to distinguish between different aspects of identity.

Social identity refers to the personality characteristics that particular cultures associate with certain social roles, e.g. in our culture, mothers are supposed to be loving, nurturing and selfless. Women who are mothers will attempt to live up to this description and, consequently, will acquire that social identity. As children grow up, they too acquire a range of social identities, e.g. brother, sister, best friend, student, etc. Interaction with others makes clear to them what our culture expects of these roles in terms of obligations, duties and behaviour.

Personal identity refers to those 'markers of individuality' (Fulcher and Scott) which identify people as distinct from others, e.g. personal name, nickname, signature, photograph, address, national insurance number, etc.

Self refers to an individual's subjective sense of his or her own identity. It is partly the product of what others expect from a person's social identity, e.g. a mother may see herself as a good mother because she achieves society's standards in that respect. However, self is also the product of how the individual interprets their own experience, e.g. some women may, in their own mind, have serious misgivings about whether they live up to society's expectations of mothers. The self, then, is the connection between social norms and the individual's interpretation of those norms.

Functionalism, culture and identity

OCR U2532

Be able to contrast this theory with Marxism.

Functionalism is a **structuralist** theory, i.e. it sees the individual as less important than the social structure of society because the individual is viewed as the **product of society**.

Functionalists believe that society exists externally to the individual, e.g. people are born into society and play a role in it. Their deaths do not mean the end of society which continues long after they are gone. Functionalists suggest that the social institutions that make up society are 'social facts' which exert a profound influence over human behaviour. Functionalists do not believe that people choose their own identities, rather these are **imposed on us by the social institutions to which we belong** which produce a value or moral consensus which provides guidelines for behaviour and therefore social order in society. For example, this concensus shapes our socialisation, through the family, education, religion and media into key values such as the importance of nuclear family life, achievement, respect for authority, etc.

Critique of functionalism

Functionalism is criticised on the grounds that it:

- presents 'an over-socialised' picture of human beings – it fails to acknowledge that culture is the product of human action and thought

- presents socialisation as a positive process that never fails. If this were the case, crime, child abuse, etc. would not be the social problems they are

- ignores the fact that power is unequally distributed in society. Some groups have more wealth and power than others and can impose their norms and values on less powerful groups.

Marxism, culture and identity

OCR U2532

Althusser rejects the functionalist view that social institutions promote a common culture and argues that cultural institutions such as the family, education, mass media and religion transmit **ruling-class norms** as 'normal' and 'natural'. The role of such institutions therefore is **ideological** because their aim is to convince members of society that their socio-economic position is deserved. This encourages **conformity**.

Be able to contrast this theory with functionalism.

> **KEY POINT**
>
> Marxists argue that culture is **the net sum of ruling-class values and norms**. Moreover, because the relationship between social classes is primarily economic, **work is the major source of identity in capitalist societies**. Social identity is dependent upon a person's **class position** and people's identities are judged according to what work they do and how much they are paid. Some members of the working class thus develop a low-status identity, e.g. they may feel deprived in terms of education and income, bored by the dead-end job they do and powerless to change their situation.

However, Marxists like functionalists neglect the view that people can choose how to behave. Marxists too rarely acknowledge the idea that people create culture.

Interpretivism, culture and identity

OCR ▶ U2532

> Note the link to labelling theory in Chapter 7.

Interpretivist theories focus on the interaction between the individual and society and suggest it is this **interaction** that creates culture and identity.

An important aspect of interpretivism is **labelling theory**. This argues that some identities are constructed by the negative reaction of others. Becker notes how the media and agents of social control such as the police and courts may, apply deviant labels to individuals acting outside the 'norm'. Deviant labels have the power of a **'master status'**, e.g. the master status of 'criminal' can override all other statuses such as father, son, etc. Becker argues that such deviant labels can radically alter social identity, e.g. someone labelled as 'criminal' may be discriminated against and thus find it difficult to regain an 'acceptable' social identity, e.g. 'worker'. They may end up seeking others with similar identities and values and form subcultures.

Interpretivist theories have been criticised because they tend to be very vague about who is responsible for defining acceptable norms of behaviour and fail to explain who is responsible for making the rules that so-called deviant groups break. They fail to explore the origin of power, and neglect potential sources such as social class, gender and ethnicity, e.g. Marxists argue that the capitalist ruling class is responsible. To summarise, interpretivist theories tend to be descriptive rather than explanatory.

Progress check

1 What is culture?

2 What are the key values of British culture according to functionalism?

3 What is an ascribed status?

4 What do structural theories believe about culture and identity?

5 What theory argues culture reflects value consensus?

6 What theory believes culture is ideological?

6 Marxism.
5 Functionalism.
4 That they are structured by factors beyond the control of the individual. Society is more important than the individual.
3 The role that one is born into.
2 Respect for human life, achievement, importance of nuclear family life, privacy, etc.
1 The way of life of a particular society.

4.2 Culture and the formation of identity

After studying this section you should be able to:

● *describe how class identity is constructed and how it influences social behaviour*
● *identify how gender-role socialisation structures gender identity*
● *describe how ethnic identities influence social behaviour*
● *outline the role of domestic and global institutions in constructing national identities*

LEARNING SUMMARY

✓ Class identity

OCR ▶ U2352

Be able to illustrate how social class shaped working-class leisure, family life, etc.

> **KEY POINT**
>
> Fulcher and Scott point out that until the late 20th century, people's identities and interests were tied up with the type of work they did and the work-based communities they lived in. In particular, the working class had a **strong sense of their social class position**. Virtually all aspects of their lives including gender roles, family life, political affiliation and leisure were a product of their keen sense of working-class identity.

Evidence for this can be found in the work of **Lockwood (1966)**, who found that many workers, especially in industrial areas, subscribed to a value system he called '**proletarian traditionalist**'. Workers felt a strong sense of loyalty to each other because of shared work experience and were thus mutually supportive, with a keen sense of class solidarity. They tended to see society in terms of conflict: 'them versus us'.

Later research has claimed that this type of class identity is in decline. **Lash and Urry (1994)** claim that there has been a '**de-centring of class identity**' for two broad reasons:

● recession and unemployment have undermined traditional working-class communities and organisations such as trade unions
● the workforce has grown more diverse. It can be divided into two broad components: the 'core' made up of secure workers with good rates of pay and promotion opportunities and the 'periphery' made up of part-time, temporary workers on short-term contracts. The entry of large numbers of women into the labour market in the 1980s onwards has added to this diversity.

Link to other studies of the working-class in other areas of the syllabus, e.g. Foster's study of East End family life.

The economic basis for class identity and solidarity has, it is argued, weakened. But this is not a new argument. Goldthorpe and Lockwood's research in the 1960s identified a '**privatised instrumentalist**' worker who saw work as a means to an end rather than as a source of identity. This type of worker was found in the newer manufacturing industries mainly situated in the South. These workers defined themselves through their families and their standard of living and had no heightened sense of class injustice.

The upper class

Although there has been limited research into how the upper class construct their social identity, it is likely that this identity is powerful. Children born into this class inherit **cultural capital** as well as economic capital. They learn distinct modes of language, mannerisms, attitudes and values which clearly **distinguish them from the masses**. The process of socialisation is reinforced by kinship, public school and Oxbridge education, membership of clubs, etc. This lifestyle usually results in a well-developed self confidence and sense of social superiority.

The middle classes

Savage's (1992) research describes three types of middle-class identity:

- Professionals subscribe to an ascetic or intellectual identity. They value cultural assets such as knowledge and qualifications, and feel it is important to pass these on to their children.

- Managers subscribe to an instrumentalist identity – they define success in terms of their standard of living and leisure pursuits.

- The entrepreneurial group works mainly in the City or in cultural organisations such as the mass media. This group subscribes to a 'post-modern' identity. This revolves around conspicuous consumption of a mixture of high and popular culture.

> Conspicuous consumption = showing off wealth and status by consuming expensive leisure products.

Consumption

OCR   U2532

> **KEY POINT**
>
> In the 1990s sociologists have argued that class has ceased to be a prime determinant of identity and that societies are now organised around consumption rather than production. People now identify themselves in terms of what they consume rather than social class position.

> Consumption cleavages = social and economic divisions created by the way goods and services are consumed.

Saunders (1990) argues that society is now characterised by a major consumption cleavage – those who mainly rely on the market for work and consumption and those who rely mainly on the State, i.e. the underclass which is workshy and welfare-dependent.

Post-modernism

Post-modernist thinkers argue that society is now media-saturated and that lifestyle for all social groups is increasingly defined by advertising and media images. Consumption no longer addresses just material needs. It is often symbolic, e.g. people may drink ice lager because it is refreshing, but also because it is fashionable.

> **KEY POINT**
>
> Post-modernists argue that class identity has fragmented into numerous separate identities. Social identity is now more pluralistic. Pakulski and Waters (1996) argue people exercise more choice about what type of people they want to be. Gender, ethnicity, age, region and family role interact and impact with consumption and media images to construct post-modern culture and identity.

However, are post-modern ideas exaggerated? Marshall's research indicates that members of a range of classes are still aware of class differences and are happy to identify themselves using class categories. Marshall does concede that workers today are largely indifferent about capitalism and therefore less likely to subscribe to 'them versus us' attitudes. Finally, post-modernists conveniently ignore that for many, consumption depends on having a job and an income, e.g. poverty is going to inhibit any desire to pursue a post-modern lifestyle, i.e. consumption and social class are closely related.

Gender identity

OCR   U2532

Sociologists distinguish between 'sex' and 'gender'. Sex describes the biological differences between males and females, e.g. chromosomes, hormones, genitals, etc. Gender refers to the cultural expectations attached to how males and females are supposed to behave. People's social status and identity will depend on their gender.

> **KEY POINT**
>
> Sociologists argue that gender is socially constructed rather than biologically determined, e.g. Lewontin (1982), a leading geneticist, said 'biological differences become the signal for, rather than a cause of, differentiation in social roles'. Feminist sociologists see gender as shaped by a social and cultural environment dominated by a **culture of patriarchy**. Gender expectations are transmitted to the next generation through **gender-role socialisation**.

From an early age, people are trained to conform to social expectations in regard to gender behaviour. Much of this training goes on in the family during primary socialisation, e.g. people use gender-oriented terms of endearment when talking to children, they dress boys and girls differently and sex-typed toys are given to children.

Oakley (1981) identifies two processes central to the construction of gender identity:

- **manipulation:** how parents encourage or discourage behaviour on the basis of appropriateness for the sex
- **canalisation:** how parents channel children's interests into toys and activities seen as normal for that sex.

These types of gender reinforcements are extremely powerful. Oakley notes that by the age of five, most children have acquired a clear gender identity. They know what gender they belong to and have a clear idea what constitutes appropriate behaviour for that gender.

Chapter 5 outlines the media's contribution to gender-role socialisation.

Other agencies of socialisation reinforce gender-role socialisation, e.g. the hidden curriculum in schools, children's books and mass media.

Walby and Pateman (1990) and Wolff (1990) note that gender-role socialisation is supported by modern society's distinction between **private and public space**. Wolff argues that women learn to be confined to the private sphere of the family and home. Public space refers to work, education and politics.

Note that sexual behaviour too involves conformity to gender expectations.

However, the idea of gender-role socialisation is criticised on the grounds that:

- the question of power is rarely addressed – why do men dominate?
- it assumes that women passively accept the gender identity imposed on them; this is an over-socialised view of women that neglects their choice in developing their own identities
- it neglects significant differences between women's experience of socialisation in terms of age, social class, ethnicity, etc.
- it neglects the fact that masculine identity may be undergoing change.

Post-modernism and gender roles

Post-modernists argue that changes in gender roles are positively impacting on female identity in three ways.

- Women's greater participation in the labour market is eroding traditional notions of female identity. Sharpe's (1994) study suggests young females are becoming more assertive about their rights to education and careers.
- Women are increasingly seeing consumption and leisure as more important than marriage and motherhood.
- Women can now pick and mix cultural styles. Some of these styles may be potentially liberating by challenging patriarchal definitions of how females are supposed to behave, e.g. the Spice Girls and 'girl power' may successfully challenge stereotyped images of femininity.

See the sections on male underachievement and deviance in Chapter 7.

> **KEY POINT**
>
> Mac En Ghaill argues that changes in the economy are leading to a 'crisis in masculinity'. The notion of protector/breadwinner may be undermined by economic change and this may be causing social problems such as domestic violence, boys' underachievement in education, and increasing suicide rates amongst young men and crime.

Think about how the film 'The Full Monty' illustrates changing masculinity.

Some commentators suggest that men may be developing more feminine qualities. Advertising stresses they should pay more attention to personal grooming. The increasing economic and social power of young women may result in some restructuring of male identity. Some commentators have suggested these processes have seen the emergence of a more caring and sensitive 'new man'. However, feminists are sceptical of this claim. The emergence of 'new lad' magazines in the last few years indicates that there may actually be a male backlash which is actively attempting to resist these processes of gender change.

Radical feminists suggest post-modernists exaggerate their arguments. They point out that there is little evidence that men and women are sharing equally in the consumption of goods and services, e.g. most media and cultural products are aimed at men. They also note that patriarchal culture is deeply embedded – consumption may be a temporary phase young single women go through before they return to the culturally expected paths of relationships and motherhood.

Ethnicity and identity

OCR ▷ U2532

Ethnicity does not mean the same as 'race'. Members of an ethnic group may share racial origin but they probably also share other cultural characteristics, e.g. history, religion, language, common geographical origin, politics, etc. All these factors shape ethnic identities. Some ethnic groups may construct a common identity and sense of community for themselves despite the fact that they are geographically dispersed, e.g. Jews.

> **KEY POINT**
>
> Miles (1989) notes that ethnicity is an important source of social identity. Membership of an ethnic group can develop a strong sense of self and others. Individuals will often make stereotypical and imagined assumptions about other ethnic groups. These function to reinforce assumptions about their own cultural identity. If a group is powerful, these assumptions may be **racist** and result in **prejudice** and **discrimination**.

Phil Cohen (1988) notes how different class sub-cultures express racism in different ways. The upper class tend to stress their superior breeding whilst working-class people practise 'territorial racism' when they see ethnic-minority culture as threatening their communities and jobs.

Ethnicity is a useful concept but it is over-simplistic to think that all ethnic minorities have the same experiences. Racism may affect ethnic identity in a number of ways:

> **KEY POINT**
>
> - Some Afro-Caribbean youth may subscribe to belief systems which are critical of white society, e.g. both the Rastafarianism and the Black Muslim movements stress white oppression of black people and black pride/power.
> - Gardner and Shukur note that young Bengalis are loyal to Islam because this provides a sense of support and positive identity denied by white culture.
> - Music, e.g. reggae, hip-hop and rap may provide positive points of identification and means of criticism for young black people.

Think about how the film 'East is East' illustrates some of these points.

There have been a number of studies of ethnic-minority culture and identity in recent years. Butler (1995) notes that young female British-Asians negotiate their associations with traditions and religion, e.g. adopting Western ideas about education and careers whilst retaining some respect for traditional religious ideas about the role of women.

Johal (1998) focuses on second- and third-generation British-Asians, noting that they have a dual identity in that they inherit an Asian identity and adopt a British one. He argues that this involves the adoption of a kind of hyper-ethnicity which involves assuming a 'white mask' in order to interact with white peers at school or college but also, whenever necessary, highlighting cultural or religious difference. He also notes that British-Asians often adopt a position of selective cultural preference – a kind of code-switching in which young Asians move between one cultural form and another.

Nationalism and identity

OCR ▸ U2532

According to Marquand, nationalism only became an important source of culture and identity with the emergence of the nation-state.

Anderson argues that nationalism is increasingly important in modern times as a source of identity. He notes that nationalism has increased in popularity in the West as religious belief has gone into decline. He argues that nationalism shares many of the functions of religion in giving people's lives meaning and promoting a sense of belonging.

Think about how British identity may be undermined by the Scottish, Welsh and Irish assemblies.

> **KEY POINT**
>
> Marquand notes that British national culture does not exist in a pure state. The British are a mix of social and immigrant groups who call themselves British. Therefore nationalism is socially constructed. It involves the inventing of traditions, symbols and mythologies to bring about a sense of national unity and identification. During the course of the 20th century, the Royal Family has played a greater national role than in previous centuries.

Schudsen (1994) notes that society's members are socialised into national culture through common language, the teaching of history, literature and religion. National rituals and mass-media focus on national institutions such as the Royal Family.

> **KEY POINT**
>
> Waters (1995) describes globalisation as a social process in which the constraints of geography on social and cultural norms and values decline. This process is believed to have a number of effects upon national cultures and identity.

- The boundaries between nation states become less significant as transnational companies and international financial markets increasingly dominate world trade. Cultural products such as films and music are produced for the international market. There are some fears that these products may erode national cultures and create an homogeneous, commercialised global culture dominated by American culture offering superficial mass entertainment.

Is there such a thing as English identity?

- National or local cultures may be strengthened as a form of resistance to globalisation. Some cultures may adopt fundamentalist (i.e. return to tradition) movements. Other societies may exaggerate aspects of their own culture in order to resist global threats, e.g. membership of Europe is seen by some as a threat to British sovereignty and its currency.

- National culture may decline, leading to new cultures and identities evolving, e.g. multicultural societies might produce **hybrid cultures** in time through inter-marriage or as second-generation members of ethnic-minority groups subscribe to values and norms from both their inherited and adopted cultures.

Progress check

1 What is a proletarian traditionalist?

2 What is a privatised individual?

3 What has allegedly replaced class as the major source of identity?

4 How are gender roles generally reinforced through school?

5 What is the crisis in masculinity?

6 What is selective cultural preference?

7 What is globalisation?

7 The process by which national boundaries are becoming less important.

6 The process by which young British-Asians switch identity according to whether they're interacting with Asian or British culture.

5 Young men's traditional sense of masculine identity is under threat from changes in the nature of work and relationships.

4 Through the 'hidden curriculum'.

3 Consumption.

2 A worker who sees work simply as a means to meet financial ends.

1 A worker who is strongly conscious of their working-class identity.

Sample question and model answer

This OCR question is worth 90 marks. You have 1 hour to do it. Allocate your time and space accordingly.

Item A

Ann Oakley made the following distinction. There are two sexes, male and female which are the result of biological differences. There are two genders which are the result of cultural differences. Sex does not determine gender. So boys fight each other not because they are male but because they have been socialised into a masculine role. Similarly, the majority of nurses are women not because they are driven to care for others by their female biology but because nursing reflects the feminine role in society. However, in the late 1980s serious questions began to be asked about gender roles. It was suggested by some that women were causing themselves stress competing with men and that masculinity was being undermined. Within feminism it became apparent that a variety of feminine and masculine roles and identities existed.

a) Identify and briefly explain, in your own words, the difference between sex and gender. [14 marks]

Questions worth 14 marks require about 5 minutes and usually demand two points to be made with illustration.

a) Sex refers to the biological or physical differences between males and females, e.g. genitalia. Gender refers to the cultural expectations associated with masculinity and femininity. For example, most nurses are female because nursing is regarded as a feminine job. It is a masculine norm for males to fight each other occasionally.

b) Identify and briefly explain two ways in which the family engages in gender-role socialisation. [14 marks]

b) Oakley refers to canalisation as the process whereby parents channel children's interests into toys and activities seen as normal for that sex. These types of gender reinforcements are extremely powerful. Gender roles may also be reinforced by parents using gender-oriented terms of endearment when talking to their children. For example, terms like 'sweet' to describe females and 'tough guy' to describe males.

c) Outline the view that masculinity is experiencing a 'crisis of identity'. [22 marks]

Spend approximately 15–20 minutes on this. Note the word 'outline' – it is asking you to describe the debate.

c) There has been a major decline in traditional male jobs and boys' perceptions of this may have influenced their motivation and ambition at school. In other words, they feel that qualifications are a waste of time because there are only limited opportunities in the job market. This may even involve constructing alternative self-esteem and status systems around delinquent or anti-school activities. Some commentators, notably Mac En Ghaill, call this a 'crisis of masculinity'. The future looks bleak and without purpose so boys don't see the point in working hard.

Other sociologists have suggested that working-class men whose identity is bound up with work and being a breadwinner may find that their traditional role and status within the family and society is undermined by unemployment. Their sense of masculinity may be further compromised if their wives become the main breadwinners. They may feel a loss of identity and role. Some may react to these profound changes in identity by attempting to re-assert masculinity through domestic violence. Others may become depressed or suicidal. Others may have to totally re-evaluate their sense of masculinity and adapt to changing circumstances, e.g. by becoming house-husbands or sharing housework and child-care.

Sample question and model answer (continued)

Spend approximately 30 minutes on this type of question. It is essentially a mini-essay of about 2 sides of A4.

d) Assess the view that it is realistic to talk about a variety of feminine roles existing in modern society. [40 marks]

d) Traditional gender-role socialisation ensures that males and females are socialised into very rigid behaviours and attitudes in regard to masculinity and femininity. For example, people use gender-oriented terms of endearment when talking to children, they dress boys and girls differently and give them sex-typed toys. Consequently, by the age of five most children have a clear gender identity.

For many years feminists were critical of gender-role socialisation because it was believed that males were socialised to see themselves as more dominant than females. Consequently, males had higher expectations in regard to education and jobs. Females were allegedly socialised into seeing themselves as the subordinate passive sex. In particular, they were supposedly encouraged to view themselves primarily as mothers and housewives. Consequently, they had lower ambitions in terms of education and careers. This is well illustrated by Sue Sharpe who in a 1976 survey discovered that girls' priorities were 'love, marriage, husbands, children, jobs and careers, more or less in that order'.

Assessment of 'traditional' gender-role socialisation.

However, there is some evidence that the women's movement may have raised the expectations of females. Many women are looking beyond the mother-housewife role as illustrated by Sharpe who repeated her research in 1994. She found that girls' priorities had changed to 'job, career and being able to support themselves'. There are also increasing job opportunities for women in the service sector of the economy. Many girls have mothers in paid employment who provide positive role models for them. As a result females now recognise that the future offers them more choices – economic independence and careers are a real possibility. These choices are reflected in the range of roles women find themselves in today. Very few women are full-time housewives. Most combine marriage, children and full-time or part-time jobs although evidence suggests that they still carry the major burden of child-care and housework. However, surveys indicate that middle-class women may be postponing marriage and children, and even putting it off altogether to pursue the material benefits of a single life.

Contemporary reference.

Post-modernists argue that changes in gender roles are positively impacting on female identity. Women are increasingly likely to see consumption and leisure as more important in the construction of their identity than domestic roles. Young women may be actively using culture in order to culturally resist patriarchal definitions of how females are supposed to behave. For example, 'girl power' may aggressively challenge traditional stereotypes of femininity.

However, we must be careful not to exaggerate the idea that a range of femininities now exist. Radical feminists point out that there is little evidence that men and women are sharing equally in the consumption of goods and services. Consumption may only be a temporary phase that young single women go through before they settle down into the culturally expected roles of marriage and motherhood.

Practice examination questions

Item A

Class has long been the main source of social identity for most people in Britain. Working-class culture, in particular, was located within localised occupational communities. On the whole, working-class culture was characterised by a shared outlook and view of the world and a common set of norms and values. Individuals gained their sense of identity from belonging to such communities. Consequently, working-class identity especially in regard to family life, leisure pursuits and voting behaviour was structured by a sense of belonging to and pride in these communities. However, in recent years, it has been suggested that such communities have been undermined by profound social and economic changes.

1 Identify and briefly explain two behaviours which Item A suggests were structured by working-class identity.   [14 marks]

2 Identify and briefly explain two social and economic changes which may be undermining working-class culture.   [14 marks]

3 What do sociological studies tell us about middle-class and upper-class identities?   [22 marks]

4 Assess the view that traditional working-class culture is on the decline.   [40 marks]

Chapter 5
Mass media

The following topics are covered in this chapter:

- Media institutions
- The effects of mass media
- Content and representation in the mass media

5.1 Media institutions

After studying this section you should be able to:

- outline and assess different sociological explanations of the relationship between ownership and control of the mass media
- compare and contrast Marxist and pluralist accounts of the media

LEARNING SUMMARY

Ownership and control

AQA   U1
OCR   U2533

Pluralism

Pluralists argue that media content is determined by the free market. If the general public did not like the content of newspapers or television programmes they would not buy or watch them. The mass media provide the public with what it wants. If the content of newspapers is biased in any way this is because newspapers reflect the political and social attitudes of their readership. Bias therefore lies with the consumer and not the owner or journalist.

Pluralists suggest that newspapers act as a watchdog to prevent abuses of power by the rich and powerful, and that investigative reporting would not exist if newspapers simply supported the interests of owners. Tunstall's survey found that journalists were mainly motivated by notions of social responsibility. In 1997 *The Guardian*'s focus on the 'Cash for Questions' scandal helped bring about the defeat of the Conservative Government of John Major. Pluralists argue this simply would not be allowed if newspapers were in the control of a political and economic élite. Instead newspapers are controlled by professionals who use their skills to make sure audiences are well catered for.

However, those criticising pluralist arguments ask how much choice really exists in the media. In 1997 only one national newspaper supported the Labour Party whilst six supported the Conservatives.

Instrumental Marxism

> Karl Marx once said 'the class which has the means of material production at its disposal has control at the same time over the production and distribution of the ideas of their age', i.e. those who own and control the media have the power to shape how we think.
>
> **KEY POINT**

Miliband is particularly critical of the pluralist argument, arguing that the political biases of a small group of media owners require capitalism and all its inequalities to continue undisturbed. This is because the political opportunities and wealth afforded to them by such a system are great. Newspapers are vehicles of the personal views of this elite and are aimed at minimising criticism of capitalism.

Evidence for the instrumental Marxist view

Know the following concepts well; concentration of ownership, conglomeration, transnationals.

It is true that ownership of newspapers in the UK is **concentrated** in the hands of six owners. Some of these control global **conglomerates** known as **transnationals** who monopolise a range of different types of media such as television and film. Ownership of international mass media is mainly concentrated in approximately 20 large corporations.

> International boundaries are increasingly ignored by **transnationals** as they seek to monopolise media in their field by buying up smaller media organisations. Governments are increasingly powerless to control the activities of such companies.
>
> **KEY POINT**

It is also true that **media owners** have interfered in the content of their newspapers, e.g. Rupert Murdoch, who owns and controls News Corp, has been accused on a number of occasions of such manipulative practices. He is quoted as saying 'I give instructions to my editors all round the world' whilst an editor of *The Times* said in 1984 of Murdoch, 'In many respects, he is the phantom Prime Minister of the country'.

However, this evidence is anecdotal. Although sociologists can prove conglomeration has occurred it is difficult, if not impossible, to prove beyond scientific doubt, that consistent manipulation of media content by owners for their own political and economic ends has occurred.

The role of editors

Always attempt to use contemporary examples.

Miliband also focuses on the role of **professional** managers and **editors**. He argues that these are given some independence by owners but ideas '**seep down**' from the top providing a framework of political ideas that editors and journalists must work within. Editors learn that there are issues which owners feel strongly about, i.e. **sacred cows**, and are under a great deal of pressure to deal with these in ways in which the owner would approve. For example, the BskyB bid for Manchester United was condemned by all newspapers except *The Sun* and The *Times*. News Corp owns all these organisations.

However, at best, most of Miliband's arguments about the media are speculative. Critics argue that news is simply the result of journalists and editors using objective news values to define what is newsworthy in terms of attracting a target or mass audience. Moreover, even if it could be proved that media manipulation exists, it is another thing altogether to prove that this has an effect upon the audience.

Hegemonic Marxism

Be willing to illustrate these ideas with reference to the Glasgow University Media Group's work on the reporting of strikes.

Hegemonic Marxists also reject the conspiratorial nature of Miliband's ideas. They argue that media content does support capitalist inequality but that this is an accidental by-product of the social backgrounds of journalists and editors and the need to attract the largest possible audience. Hegemonic Marxists point out that journalists are recruited from a narrow social background and tend to be middle-class, white and male. They therefore subscribe to news' values which stress a consensus or middle-of-the-road view of society (*weltanschauung*). Journalists will avoid extreme or 'threatening' ideas in order not to lose readers. The focus on entertainment at the expense of news is simply a way of achieving large audiences and so the media very rarely challenge the established order. Hegemonic Marxists conclude that news is largely the product of professional practices and the unconscious biases of journalists and professional managers rather than a deliberate conspiracy by owners.

Progress check

1 Who argue that media content is not manipulated by owners?

2 Who said that the class that controls wealth is likely to control ideas and knowledge?

3 Which theory claims that owners exercise deliberate ideological control over the media?

4 What is a transnational?

5 What does Miliband mean by a 'sacred cow'?

6 What does hegemony mean?

7 What does *weltanschauung* mean?

7 One world view which is shared by the majority of middle-class white male journalists.
6 Cultural dominance of middle-class ideas.
5 An issue on which owners have strong opinions and on which editors are expected to toe a certain line.
4 Global companies that operate across national boundaries, e.g. News Corp.
3 Instrumental Marxism.
2 Marx.
1 Pluralists.

5.2 The effects of mass media

After studying this section you should be able to:

- *assess the view that the mass media exerts an imitative effect upon young audiences*
- *evaluate the view that the mass media propagates mass culture*
- *describe post-modern developments in media use*

LEARNING SUMMARY

Theories of mass media effects

AQA ▶ U1
OCR ▶ U2533

The hypodermic-syringe model

> The hypodermic-syringe model is typical of early research into media effects upon audiences. Essentially it sees a cause and effect relationship between a passive and homogeneous audience and an active media. It is argued that children and impressionable adults are negatively influenced by sex and violence, especially on television and in films, and this may lead to imitation in the form of violent crime.
>
> KEY POINT

Sociological research is used to support this model. In the 1970s, Belson's survey of over 1000 teenage boys in London claimed that boys with high exposure to violence on television are more likely to commit violent acts. He argued that boys saw violence as a legitimate problem-solving device because their television heroes used it. However, Belson's methodology was criticised, e.g. the survey relied on self-reports (which are notoriously unreliable because of the potential for exaggeration). Moreover, Belson took responsibility for defining what counted as a violent programme, and there is some evidence that his definitions did not equate with those of the boys.

> The debate is on-going and you should illustrate with contemporary examples.

> In the 1990s the hypodermic-syringe model was modified by Elizabeth Newson. She argues that prolonged exposure to violent programmes leads to a 'drip' effect. She claims that exposure to violence over the long term in the early socialisation years leads to children using aggression rather than negotiation to solve conflicts. She concludes that violence in society continues to be a problem because poor parenting by some sections of society means that children have open access to unsuitable programmes.
>
> KEY POINT

The hypodermic-syringe model has been influential and led to the banning of video nasties in the early 1980s, the 9 pm watershed on television and pressure to severely censor films and videos for violence and bad language.

However, methodologically the model is very weak because:

- it ignores the fact that the social characteristics of audiences differ in terms of age, class, gender, ethnicity, etc.
- Murdock and McCron note that it often ignores the social context of violence. Violence may be the product of gender-role socialisation, the alienating experience of education, work, unemployment, urbanisation and the influence of the peer group, etc. In other words, media content is only one variable amongst many.
- Barker (1996) argues it sees audiences as 'cultural dopes', whereas in reality they are very active in how they use the media. He claims that people are intelligent enough to understand that imitation of violent television is socially unacceptable.

The selective filter model of media

The hypodermic-syringe model ignores the fact that audiences give varying amounts of attention to the media. **Klapper's 'selective filter'** model of media argues that audiences actively use the media and that before media content can have any effect upon an audience it must go through three filters.

* First, **selective exposure** – people must choose to access the media. Klapper points out that what is accessed may depend on parental control, education and interest. People tend to choose programmes which confirm their existing tastes, values and prejudices and are not generally interested in programmes which aim to change their ideas.

* Second, Klapper highlights **selective perception** – people interpret the same programmes in different ways and may choose to ignore its messages.

* Third, **selective retention** – people only remember media content that supports their beliefs.

> Klapper argues that sociologists should think about **what audiences do with the media** rather than what the media does to the audience. Reducing social behaviour to simple cause and effect relationships, i.e. television causes anti-social behaviour, underestimates the complexities of social behaviour.
>
> **KEY POINT**

Uses and gratifications theory

Think about the function of soap operas, catharsis = release of emotions.

Blumler and McQuail's 'Uses and Gratifications' theory of media focuses on how the audience uses the media in different ways to gratify social needs such as companionship, community, escape from routine, education, catharsis, family interaction, etc. It points out that different social groups have varying social needs and therefore use the media differently. However, Blumler and McQuail have been accused of being overly romantic about the functions of the media and of ignoring its potential **dysfunctions**. Marxists, for example, argue that it ignores the possibility that social needs are **'false needs'** created by capitalism to detract from class inequalities.

> There is still no overwhelming evidence that media content influences audiences. **Newburn and Hagell's** 1995 review of all research in this field found no evidence of a direct causal relationship between media and violence. Their own survey found little difference in the viewing habits of their delinquent and non-delinquent sample.
>
> **KEY POINT**

The emphasis in sociological research is now moving away from looking at the media's influence over behaviour. Recent studies, e.g. **Morley, Buckingham,** etc., have focused on **'reception analysis'** – how different audiences interpret media according to their social class, age, gender, ethnicity, etc.

Cultural effects theory

AQA   U1
OCR   U2533

The idea that the mass media have created a mass culture in society is particularly associated with Marxism – especially **Marcuse**, who sees the mass media as part of a **'culture industry'**. The ideological function of this industry is to reproduce class inequality by bringing about the false class-consciousness of the working class.

However, the mass culture argument is also associated with New Right thinkers who argue that a 'dumbed-down' mass media has replaced the family and religion as the main source of culture and morality. Active audiences who once interacted with each other have been turned into antisocial couch potatoes.

Marxists such as **Marcuse** argue that pre-industrial popular culture or folk culture was the product of the family and revolved around folk music, dancing, folk tales, carnivals, etc. However, in capitalist society, popular culture is no longer the product of the people, but rather a product of commercial pressures and mass production. In particular, mass or popular culture mainly revolves around Hollywood, commercial television, tabloid newspapers, pop music and advertising.

> **KEY POINT**
>
> Marcuse argued that this type of **popular culture** is responsible for stifling creativity, imagination and critical thought in society. It is a modern day 'opium of the people' or **ideology** which serves to disguise the true extent of working-class exploitation by the capitalist class. Marcuse was particularly critical of advertising, which he argued plays a key role in encouraging the working class to passively accept inequality. It does this by encouraging them to see their lives satisfied by the fulfilment of **'false needs'** through acquiring consumer items. Thus, the mass media play a major role in reproducing, maintaining and legitimating class inequality.

Marcuse's views are similar to those of the 'romantic-right' who argue that the growing popularity of a 'plastic commodity culture' means people have become passive recipients of culture rather than active participants in it. Consequently, people internalise violent images from Hollywood films – children and impressionable young people may be at risk from this. Advertising gives people an appetite for things they cannot have and therefore fuels crime.

There are a number of criticisms of the mass-culture argument:

- It is élitist and smacks of intellectual arrogance, implying that popular culture is trivial and has little or no value.

- It assumes that, having been culturally duped, the masses have inferior tastes – a rather ethnocentric and over-socialised view of human beings. In many ways, this mass-culture theory is similar to the hypodermic-syringe model of media effects. Like that model, it is difficult to 'prove' an effect.

- Pluralists argue that pre-industrial folk culture has been over-romanticised by these critics.

- Pluralists also argue that the mass media in modern societies has had many positive effects – encouraging literacy and making people more aware of the world around them. People have much more choice of opinion and cultural products than ever before.

Post-modernism and the media

AQA U1
OCR U2533

> **KEY POINT**
>
> It has been suggested that capitalism has now entered a new stage of development known as **post-modernism**. In particular, the globalisation of mass media, information technology and electronic communication such as e-mail and the Internet has led to the decline of national cultures and the growing importance of cultural diversity on our lifestyles.

Strinati (1995) argues that the mass media is pivotal in the development of post-modern society for two major reasons:

- The media increasingly defines our lifestyles and identity for us, e.g. Strinati notes that the media (via television) tell us what our homes and gardens should look like. Advertising tells us what commodities we need in order to improve the quality of our lives. Magazines tell us how we can become attractive to the opposite sex. News tells us what issues we should be thinking about. Docu-soaps reassure us that other people share our anxieties, and so on.

- In the post-modern world we learn through the media that consumption of images and signs for their own sake is more important than the consumption of the goods they represent, i.e. style is more important than content. We buy the labels and packaging rather than the clothes and goods themselves.

Progress check

1 What is an homogeneous audience?

2 Who invented the 'drip theory' of media effects?

3 How do Murdock and McCron criticise the hypodermic-syringe model?

4 What does cultural doping refer to?

5 Identify Klapper's three selective filters.

6 How does Marcuse see popular culture?

7 According to post-modernism, what is the most important influence on people's identity and lifestyle today?

7 The mass media.
6 As an ideology stifling critical thinking.
5 Exposure, perception and retention.
4 The view of the audience as overly passive and lacking the intelligence to distinguish between reality and fantasy.
3 They say it ignores the social context of violence, i.e. family background, influence of peer group, etc.
2 Elizabeth Newson.
1 One that shares the same characteristics.

5.3 Content and representation in the mass media

After studying this section you should be able to:

- *outline the role of media professionals in constructing the news*
- *describe the role of the mass media in representations of gender, ethnicity, social class and age*

The social construction of news

AQA	U1
OCR	U2533

Questions about news are popular!

Interactionists argue that thousands of news events happen every day but only a dozen or so are selected for television news and newspapers – thus the news does not reflect social reality but rather the professional practices of journalists and editors who use their expertise to socially construct the news on our behalf.

News-gathering is a selective process. Journalists and editors make choices about what news to cover and how to cover it. Three key concepts are important in understanding how news is socially constructed or manufactured:

- **Gate-keepers** are the media personnel, such as editors and journalists, involved in the selection of news. They open the gate to some stories whilst closing the gate for others.

- **Agenda-setting** refers to how editors, journalists and broadcasters prioritise and filter what to include and what not to include. This depends on what type of media organisation is involved in news selection. The agenda of television news tends to be different to newspapers. Tabloid newspapers may have a different agenda to broadsheets. Agenda setting is dependent upon practical constraints, e.g. the amount of space or time, whether it is possible to transmit live pictures, photographs, etc.

> **KEY POINT**
>
> **News values** are used by journalists to define stories as 'newsworthy' or interesting enough to grab a large audience.
>
> News stories that are dramatic (e.g. war), unexpected, and unambiguous (i.e. easy to explain) are more likely to be selected. Complex stories which can be reduced to personalities (e.g. evil Saddam Hussein) or which involve élite nations or celebrities are more likely to be reported. Bad news is generally regarded by journalists as more exciting than good news.

Interactionists regard news values as the product of economic pressures, i.e. the media needs to attract an audience in order to generate sales and advertising revenue. Marxists, on the other hand, link news production to ownership and control issues – arguing that news is selected in line with capitalist interests. Any news that challenges the status quo will be filtered out of the news-gathering process.

Representations of women in the media

AQA	U1
OCR	U2533

Sociological research suggests that stereotypical images of women persist across a range of media, as described below.

- Women are portrayed in a narrower range of social roles than men. They are still to be found mainly in domestic settings, e.g. **Cumberbatch's** 1990 study of advertising found that women were twice as likely to engage in household labour than men. Men were also twice as likely than women to be represented in paid employment.

This material is also useful for illustrating the process of gender-role socialisation in Chapter 4.

- When women are portrayed as career women there is a tendency to depict them as unfulfilled, unattractive, unstable and unable to sustain a satisfactory family life.

- Women are still depicted as sex objects, e.g. Cumberbatch's survey found that women more often occupy a decorative role than men. Mulvey has expressed concern at the **objectivation** of women's bodies in films as sexual objects to be enjoyed by men. Most women on television and in films tend to be aged under 30 years. Physical looks, sex appeal and youth seem to be a necessary social attribute for women but less important for male film-stars and television presenters/newscasters.

- Cumberbatch found that men outnumber women by a ratio of 2:1 in advertising whilst 89% of voice-overs for television commercials were male.

- There is also evidence that female issues are **marginalised** by the media. Most newspapers have 'women's pages' which focus on women as a special group with special needs which are frequently defined as emotional. Female sport also is marginalised in both newspapers and on television. Feminist ideas and lesbianism are often treated critically or excluded altogether with the media suggesting these groups are a fanatical minority.

The pluralist explanation

Pluralists believe the mass media reflects the role of women in society rather than creates these stereotypical images. They argue that sexist stereotyping in the media is in decline because social attitudes towards women's issues are changing for the better. Representations of women now reflect the changing role of women in the economy and at work and their increased spending power. Moreover, those who produce media content have become more liberal and feminised. Pluralists point to the increasing number of journalists, editors, TV writers, directors and producers who are female and argue that strong female characters are appearing in soap-operas and dramas such as 'Prime Suspect'.

Feminist explanations

This debate is on-going. There are often articles in the broadsheets on how women are treated in the media.

Liberal Feminists are sympathetic to Pluralist arguments. They agree that traditional representations of women are being challenged, although they acknowledge that there exists a cultural lag. Media images of women are slow to change in response to real social changes. However, liberal feminists are generally optimistic that positive change is occurring.

Radical feminists see the mass media, along with other patriarchal institutions such as the family, as responsible for creating stereotypical images of women. They argue that the function of the mass media is to reproduce, maintain and legitimate male power. Men dominate top positions throughout the media and use these to transmit exploitative images of women. Such images confirm for women that their primary role is mother–housewife or sex object and that they should not challenge men for jobs and careers. The media's role therefore is to celebrate the traditional female role and criticise those women who reject it.

Remember, examiners want to see recent evidence.

The evidence does suggest that women are under-represented in senior roles in the media, e.g. in 1996 only 4 out of 30 top BBC executives were female and in 1996 only 20% of newspaper editors were women. Women made up only 17% of journalists on national newspapers. However, radical feminists can be criticised for being over-deterministic. They assume that women are cultural dopes successfully persuaded by the media and other agencies to occupy subordinate roles. The educational success of females since the 1980s indicates resistance to media stereotyping.

Socialist feminists argue that mass-media organisations are capitalist enterprises which aim to make profit and in order to do so need to attract the largest possible audience. Media organisations are dominated by men and so media content is structured by male perspectives on what will attract mass audiences. The proven attractions or lowest common denominators are sitcoms, soap-operas, game shows, sex, scandal and sport. Traditional images of women are seen as 'normal' within these media formats whilst feminist images are seen as turning audiences off. In this sense, then, the media creates stereotypical images of women in order to attract audiences. These images are exaggerated but probably do reflect reality in that society is not yet characterised by gender equality.

Representations of race and ethnicity

AQA U1
OCR U2

There is recent evidence that tabloid newspapers have transferred these concerns to East European refugees.

There is evidence that some elements of the mass media show ethnic minorities in stereotypical roles:

- Tabloid newspapers have often created moral panics around issues such as immigration and alleged abuse of the welfare state. In these contexts, ethnic minorities are often represented as a threat.
- Van Dijk's (1991) study of European newspaper coverage indicates that black people are often portrayed as criminal and as drug users. Hall's study of newspaper coverage of mugging in the early 1970s supports this view.
- Issues which directly affect black people in the UK such as racist attacks, poor housing, unemployment, policing, prejudice and discrimination, etc., are very rarely heard in the media, e.g. inner-city riots are often dismissed as the product of criminality rather than frustration at institutional racism.
- Stories about the Third World tend to focus on a 'coup–war–famine–starvation syndrome'. Black people in poor countries are often portrayed as in need of Western help and the role of the West in perpetuating Third World poverty is neglected.
- Surveys of television programmes, advertising and films indicate that black people are under-represented in terms of roles.

Explanations

> - Pluralists argue that media content reflects social reality, that racist stereotyping is a thing of the past and that black role models are on the increase.
> - Hartmann and Husband blame news values which stress the newsworthiness of bad news and stories about conflict. Stereotypical stories about crime and immigration will sell more newspapers than complex stories about discriminatory practices in employment and housing.
> - Marxists argue that racist imagery of black people in the media ensures that the black and white working class remains divided. The white working class are encouraged to blame black people for lack of jobs, etc., rather than the capitalist system.

KEY POINT

Representations of class

AQA U1
OCR U2533

There have been few studies of the representation of class in the media. However, content analysis studies by **Glennon and Butsch (1982)** and **Jhally and Lewis** indicate that working-class people are under-represented on television in family dramas and sitcoms. The majority of leading characters on television, especially in the USA, are middle-class males. However, working-class culture is usually dealt with positively by soap-operas such as 'EastEnders' and 'Coronation Street'.

Studies of social class in non-fictional contexts indicate that working-class people may generally be getting a poor press, e.g. **Glasgow University Media Group**'s study of the media's reporting of industrial disputes suggests that working-class employees were generally portrayed as 'trouble'. Studies of working-class youth culture generally conclude that these have been demonised by media '**moral panics**'.

Representations of age

AQA U1

Look at the section on youth and moral panics in Chapter 7.

Pearson's analysis of media reporting of the young suggests that they have always been represented as a '**problem**'. The work of **Cohen and Young** on 1960s youth cultures suggests that the media focused on labelling young people who played an active part in these groups as **folk devils** in need of social control. Such moral panics are inevitably linked to notions of moral decline and Marxists see them as serving an ideological function. Young people are scapegoated by society for social problems caused by the mismanagement of capitalism.

Signorelli's (1984) content analysis of American television concludes that the young were often portrayed as violent. Elderly men were more likely to be seen in a comic role whilst older women were most likely to be seen as victims. However, British research by **Lambert** *et al.* (1984) suggests that the elderly are portrayed positively on British television. On the other hand, Age Concern's campaign against ageism in 1993 criticised newspaper coverage of the elderly as reinforcing negative stereotypes.

Progress check

1 Who act as gate-keepers in regard to access to the news?

2 What is agenda-setting?

3 What are news values?

4 Which two theories claim that stereotyping of women in the media mirrors the treatment of women in society?

5 What theory claims that the sexist portrayal of women in the media is an accidental by-product of the need to make profit?

6 What do Hartmann and Husband blame for racist stereotypes in the media?

7 Who or what does Marxism blame for media racism?

7 The capitalist system.
6 News values that stress bad news and conflict.
5 Hegemonic Marxism.
4 Pluralism and Liberal Feminism.
3 The criteria journalists use to work out whether a story is newsworthy, i.e. will attract a large audience.
2 The prioritising of news items. Some are regarded as more important than others.
1 Editors and journalists, sometimes owners and governments.

Sample question and model answer

A typical OCR question. Spend 15 minutes on part a).

a) Identify and explain two ways in which the consumption of mass media has changed in the last decade?   [20 marks]

a) In post-modern society the media is responsible for undermining our sense of time and space. It used to be the case that we were largely confined to our own societies and time-zones. However, advances in media technology mean that we now live in a 'global village'. Satellite broadcasting and the Internet have produced instantaneous images and information. In the comfort of our living rooms we watched the Gulf War 'live' on CNN. Moreover, the Internet allows us cyber-access to anywhere in the world.

There are now signs that consumption patterns are changing because of the Internet. For example, we can use this technology to shop and bank, to buy stocks and shares, to gamble and to send greeting cards without having to leave the comfort of our homes.

Spend 30 minutes on part b).

b) Outline and assess the view that the mass media have created a mass culture.
                    [40 marks]

Outline first.

b) Marxists such as Marcuse argued that pre-industrial popular culture revolved around folk music, dancing, folk tales, carnivals, etc. However, in capitalist society, popular culture is no longer the product of the people. Rather it is a product of commercial pressures and mass production. In particular, mass or popular culture mainly revolves around Hollywood, commercial television, tabloid newspapers, pop music and advertising. Marcuse argues popular culture is a modern-day 'opium of the people' because it encourages the population to be more interested in entertainment such as soap operas, TV stars, football, Royalty, etc. rather than thinking critically about how they could improve their lot.

Assessment.

Marcuse has been accused of élitism and intellectual arrogance. He implies that high culture (e.g. classical music, Shakespeare, etc.) is good for us and that popular culture is trivial and has little or no value. This is, of course, a rather ethnocentric and over-generalised view.

Assessment.

Pluralists reject the view that mass culture is necessarily shallow and superficial and argue that pre-industrial folk culture has been over-romanticised by these critics. Life for many working-class people in pre-industrial times was often nasty, brutish and short. People rarely had contact with culture of any sort. Pluralists also argue that the mass media in modern societies has had many positive effects. It has encouraged literacy and made people much more aware of the world around them. People have much more choice of opinion and cultural products than ever before.

Contemporary conclusion.

Despite these criticisms, post-modernists such as Strinati have raised concerns about the role of the media. He argues that what we take as 'real' is to a great extent what the media tell us is real. Consequently the media defines our lifestyles and identity for us. In the post-modern world we also learn that style is more important than substance. We buy the labels and packaging rather than the clothes and goods themselves. In post-modern society therefore, our identities are increasingly structured by our consumption patterns rather than our social class, gender or ethnicity.

Practice examination questions

Item A

Martin Barker dismisses the concept of the stereotype as a 'useless tool for investigating media texts'. His main objection is that stereotypes are condemned for both misrepresenting the 'real world', e.g. for reinforcing the (false) stereotype that women are available for sex at any time, and for being too close to the 'real world', e.g. for showing women mainly in the home and servicing men – which many in fact do. However, despite Barker's objections, stereotypical judgements are made by everyone as part of creating order out of everyday life; as well as providing a sense of group identity. Media representations therefore may serve to inform, reinforce or challenge such stereotypes.

Source: Adapted from Tim O'Sullivan et al. Studying The Media: An Introduction, *Arnold, 1994*

Item B

Ownership of private media is now largely in the hands of multinational corporations. It is argued that such concentrated private ownership is naturally at odds with public interest. It is often argued that proprietors use their properties to restrict the flow of information and debate on which democracy depends. These fears were fuelled by the rise of the great press barons at the turn of the century who had no qualms about using their large circulations to promote their pet political causes or to put down those they disagreed with. The rise of communications conglomerates, encouraged by privatisation, deregulation and the development of global technologies is seen by some as dangerous to democracy. However, the production of communications is not merely a reflection of owners but is also subject to media professionals who produce the words, images and news on a daily basis.

Source: Adapted from Steve Taylor (ed.), Sociology: Issues and Debates, *Macmillan, 1999*

1   Explain what is meant by representation.   [2 marks]

2   Suggest two reasons why ownership of the mass media has become increasingly concentrated in the last ten years.   [4 marks]

3   Identify three ways in which media representations have reinforced stereotypes of ethnic minorities.   [6 marks]

4   Identify and briefly describe two criticisms of the view that proprietors use their power to restrict information and debate.   [8 marks]

5   Outline the view that media professionals are more important than owners in the production of news.   [20 marks]

6   Using material from Item A and other sources, evaluate the view that media representations of women challenge gender stereotypes.   [20 marks]

Chapter 6

Religion

The following topics are covered in this chapter:

- *Religious institutions*
- *The influence of religion on the individual and society*
- *Religion and classical sociology*

6.1 Religious institutions

LEARNING SUMMARY

After studying this section you should be able to:

- *distinguish between different religious institutions and outline their relationship to society and each other*
- *identify different explanations of religious innovation and renewal*

Types of religious organisation

OCR U2533

Sociologists have constructed 'ideal types' of religious organisation covering the major forms of religious activity.

Church

E.g. the Church of England.

This is a stable, formal organisation with a hierarchy and bureaucracy of paid officials, and widely accepted beliefs and values. It may be involved in some secular concerns such as education and tends to have a close relationship with the State and Monarchy. Although all sections of the population are represented in its members, the higher status groups tend to be over-represented. Worship tends to be formal and ritualised, and conducted by ordained clerics.

Denomination

E.g. Methodism.

This organisation also has beliefs and values which are widely accepted, but it has no formal connection with the State. Worship is less formal. Hierarchy and bureaucracy are less developed. Lay-persons are encouraged to lead worship.

Sect

KEY POINT

A sect is an organisation whose members join it of their own free will. It may be led by a charismatic leader and sect members tend to believe in the superiority of their group. They are the chosen ones who are 'saved', 'enlightened' or have experienced the 'truth'. Sect beliefs tend to conflict with those of society. Sects are generally insular and make strong claims on the loyalty of their members. Sects often attempt to repress individuality – in some, new members are encouraged to take on a new name and contact with family and friends is restricted. Personal responsibility may be surrendered and little opportunity given for freedom of thought.

Cult

Cults share many of the characteristics of sects. However, cults are different in that people normally join to achieve some practical end. Cults do not usually challenge social norms and usually appeal to the socially privileged. **Stark and Bainbridge (1985)** distinguish between:

- 'audience cults' which tend to be unorganised, e.g. astrology
- 'client cults' which are organised to provide a service, e.g. Spiritualism, and
- 'cultic movements' which offer spiritual and material supports to their members.

New religious movements (NRMs)

OCR ▶ U2533

Roy Wallis claims that NRMs are generally distinct from sects and cults. He argues there are three general types:

- **World-rejecting** NRMs reject the secular world as corrupt and beyond redemption. Such NRMs either abandon the world or attempt to transform the world with evangelical zeal. For example, the Unification Church, commonly known as the Moonies, rejects materialism, encourages its members to hand over all assets and imposes an ascetic lifestyle on its followers.

- **World-affirming** NRMs accept the values and goals of wider society but aim to provide a new means to achieve these. Human beings are seen as having enormous physical, mental and spiritual potential. These NRMs advertise themselves as an alternative way of achieving economic and social success. Such sects usually involve some financial investment and their recruits mainly originate in the middle class, e.g. scientology.

- **World-accommodating** NRMs neither fully accept the values and goals of wider society nor do they entirely reject society. These NRMs exist on the margins of established churches and denominations. They are a response to the increasing secularisation of the institutional church. The 'New Evangelical Movement' made up of fundamentalist, 'born again' Christian groups have grown rapidly in numbers in recent years and are typical of this type of NRM.

New Age movements (NAMs)

NAMs are similar to cults – many are simply consumer-oriented, e.g. selling products such as music, herbal remedies, etc. Others are more organised and concerned with the selling of specific messages such as opposition to traditional scientific approaches, an emphasis on green issues like environmentalism and/or vegetarianism, and a focus on spiritual and personal empowerment. **Healas (1996)** suggests that NAMs contain elements of world-rejecting counter-culture in their focus on the 'alternative' and yet they subscribe to the commercialism of the mainstream market-place.

Why people join sects

Sects may be evidence of disillusion with institutionalised religion and may result from a search for more genuine ways of satisfying spiritual needs.

> **Max Weber** linked sects to social stratification. Sects are most likely to emerge amongst the poor. Such groups may develop a 'theodicy of disprivilege' – a religious set of ideas which explains why they are in that position. For example, if a group believes that they are 'God's chosen people', the promise of 'salvation' is 'compensation' for their poverty.

KEY POINT

Questions on sects tend to focus on how they differ from mainstream religion and their relationship to social change.

However, sects also attract members of the middle classes. **Glock and Stark** use the concept of **relative deprivation** to explain this – some members of the middle class may feel relatively deprived compared with other groups. Glock and Stark identify a number of different types of relative deprivation:

- **Social deprivation** may stem from a lack of power, prestige and status. For example, those lacking job satisfaction may find alternative sources of satisfaction in the evangelical goals set by conversionist sects such as Jehovah's Witnesses, Mormons, etc.

- **Organismic deprivation** is experienced by those who suffer physical and mental problems, e.g. people may turn to sects in the hope of being healed or as an alternative to drugs or alcohol.

- **Ethical deprivation** is the result of people perceiving the world to be in moral decline and therefore retreating into an introversionist sect, e.g. Jim Jones' People's Temple or David Koresh's Branch Davidian sect.

- **Psychic deprivation** refers to those searching for more than the dominant value system offers. They may wish for inner spiritual fulfillment rather than the consumerist goals on offer in capitalist societies. Certain sects, e.g. the Divine Light Mission, Transcendental Meditation (TM), Moonies, etc., claim to offer this. Such cults tend to be attractive to the middle class and the young.

> Closely related to the concept of relative deprivation is the idea that religious sects are the product of social change. Such change may create the conditions for various forms of deprivation.
>
> **KEY POINT**

Note that social change is strongly linked to various types of deprivation.

- **Wilson** argues that the popularity of religious sects in the late 18th and early 19th centuries, both in the UK and USA, was a reaction to anxieties created by **industrialisation** and **urbanisation**.

- 20th-century sects may be a response to anxieties created by the dominance of **scientific rationalism**, **materialism** and the resulting **secularisation** of society.

- **Robert Bellah** argues that the increase in sect and cult membership seen in the late 1960s in the USA was due to middle-class youth experiencing a 'crisis of meaning' in regard to the materialistic values of their parent's culture. Many turned to an alternative drug/pop culture which rejected such values. This youth culture burnt itself out at the end of the 1960s. Sects based on anti-materialist and 'free love' values such as The Jesus People and the Children of God, and Eastern-influenced NRMs such as the Hare Krishna and the Moonies, recruited in large numbers from young people in search of spiritual or psychic goals.

The **future** of sects is difficult to predict. Some may die out when their charismatic leader dies or because children of sect members are not as committed to the belief system. They may destroy themselves (e.g. Jim Jones' People's Temple committed mass suicide). They may be destroyed by society because society dislikes and fears the superior attitude of these groups (e.g. David Koresh's Branch Davidian sect in Waco, Texas was wiped out in a fire after law enforcement agencies besieged their compound). However, some will flourish. World-affirming NRMs attract a great deal of wealth. Some may become so popular that they evolve into denominations and churches. Some of the born-again Christian movements have gone this way.

Progress check

1 What is a theodicy of disprivilege?

2 What is organismic deprivation?

3 What is ethical deprivation?

4 What was the main reason, according to Wilson, for sect growth in the 18th and 19th centuries?

5 What was the main cause of sect growth in the 1960s and 1970s?

5 The search for meaning (psychic deprivation) experienced by educated middle-class youth.
4 The anxiety created by social change, specifically industrialisation and urbanisation.
3 A feeling that the world is in moral decline. A sect might be joined in order to combat this.
2 Experience of physical or mental problems which may act as a motivation for joining a sect.
1 A set of ideas that rationalises poverty by suggesting that those who experience it are chosen by God.

6.2 The influence of religion on the individual and society

After studying this section you should be able to:

- identify the different arguments in the secularisation debate
- outline the basis of religious fundamentalism
- demonstrate how ethnicity and gender interact with religious belief

LEARNING SUMMARY

The secularisation debate

OCR   U2533

Bryan Wilson argues that secularisation is the process by which religious institutions, actions and practices lose their social significance. There are four key elements to his argument.

Statistical evidence

This material is excellent for illustrating the use of statistics in sociological research.

> Wilson focuses on **statistical evidence** relating to religious institutions and their activity. The strongest evidence for secularisation in the UK comes from church attendance statistics. According to the 1851 Census approximately 40% of the population attended church. By 1990 this had dropped to 10% according to **Brierley**. Attendance at religious ceremonies such as baptisms, communion and confirmation have also dramatically fallen. Wilson, like the New Right, sees the decline in church marriages (down to 53% in 1990), the rising divorce rate and the increase in cohabitation and number of children born outside marriage as evidence that religion and its moral value system exerts little influence today.
>
> KEY POINT

However, **interpretivist sociologists** suggest these statistics should be treated with caution for the following reasons.

- Statistics relating to the previous century are probably unreliable because sophisticated data-collection practices were not in place.

- Contemporary statistics may also be unreliable because different religious organisations employ different counting methods.

- Bellah argues that people who attend church are not necessarily practising religious belief and those who do believe may not see the need to attend. Religion is a private experience for many and consequently cannot be reliably or scientifically measured.

- The statistical evidence available is contradictory. Membership of NRMs has risen substantially in the last ten years especially amongst the young. The number of ethnic-minority religions in the UK has also increased, e.g. the number of Muslims now outnumbers the number of Methodists by 2:1.

In conclusion, critics of Wilson point out that the statistical evidence only measures **participation in institutionalised religion** rather than **religious belief**.

The growth of rationalism

> Wilson suggests that rational thinking in the shape of science has replaced religious influence in our lives because scientific progress has resulted in higher living standards. Moreover, science has produced convincing explanations for phenomena which were once the province of religion, e.g. how the world was created, etc. People have therefore become increasingly '**disenchanted**' with religion.
>
> **KEY POINT**

Critics of Wilson argue that:

Disenchantment is sometimes referred to as the de-sacrilisation of religion.

- He may be over-emphasising the influence of rationality. There is evidence that people prefer 'religious' explanations for random events like the early death of loved ones, e.g. 'God has taken them', etc.

- Many people subscribe to quasi-religious concepts like 'luck' or 'fate'.

- Social attitude surveys indicate a continuing strong belief in God.

- People's belief in science also depends on irrational faith. People don't often see the empirical evidence for science or understand it but accept it without question because scientists have been elevated to high-priest status.

Disengagement of the Church from society

> Wilson argues that the church is no longer involved in important areas of social life such as politics, and politicians don't ensure their policies meet with the approval of religious leaders. People are more likely to take moral direction from the mass media than the church. Public apathy to religion now means that it only has **symbolic value** today, with people only entering church for 'hatching, matching and dispatching' ceremonies. Wilson concludes that the Church occupies a marginal status in modern society.
>
> **KEY POINT**

Critics of Wilson argue the following:

- Religion is still a major provider of education and welfare for the poor.

- The media still shows a great interest in religious issues such as women priests.

- National religious ceremonies such as the funeral of Diana, Princess of Wales suggest that the sacred might still be important.

- Some sociologists (notably Parsons) say that disengagement is probably a good thing because it means that the churches can focus more effectively on their central role of providing moral goals for society to achieve.

Religious pluralism

Another aspect of secularisation identified by Wilson is religious pluralism. The established church no longer ministers to all members of society. Instead, as **Bruce** argues, industrialisation has fragmented society into a market-place of religions. Wilson argues that competition between religions undermines their credibility and they can no longer take loyalty for granted as they compete for 'spiritual shoppers'. Religion thus no longer acts as an integrating force in society.

> Secularisation = a form of social change which is responsible for increases in sect membership.

In particular, the growth in the number of sects, cults and new religious movements is cited by Wilson as evidence of secularisation. He argues that sects are the last outpost of religion in a secular society and are a symptom of religion's decline. He suggests that members of sects are only temporarily committed to religious beliefs and are more committed to following a charismatic leader or attracted by the lifestyle. He sees sects as being short-lived with members drifting in and out of them.

However, studies by **Greely and Nelson** argue that the growth of new religious movements indicates that society is undergoing a religious revival. G.K. Nelson agrees with Wilson that established religion is undergoing secularisation. The young, in particular, are 'turned-off' by overly bureaucratic and formal religion. However, Nelson argues that a religious revival is underway in evangelical circles, where churches offer a more spontaneous religion less reliant on ritual and consequently more attractive to the young.

> Conclusions.

Profound changes are clearly occurring in institutional religion in the UK. However, whether these changes can be described as secularisation is difficult to ascertain. A major problem is that sociologists cannot agree on a universal definition of religious belief and therefore secularisation. At best the evidence is mixed. **Stark and Bainbridge** argue that secularisation is probably a cyclical process and we are now passing out of a period of low religious belief into an upswing as we anxiously enter the 21st century. In conclusion, it may be that religion is merely changing and adapting rather than being in decline.

Religious fundamentalism

OCR ▸ U2533

Bird (1999) defines religious fundamentalism 'as a form of religious belief and practice which argues that we need to return to a time when religion was more important'. Religion is seen to provide 'definitive answers to moral problems and questions of right and wrong'.

Fundamentalist movements, whether Western or non-Western, have a great deal in common. They are likely to wish for a return to moral certainty and see the collapse of community in the modern world as responsible for social problems such as crime.

Religion and ethnicity

OCR ▸ U2533

Madood and Berthold's survey (1994) of religious affiliation among ethnic-minority groups indicates that they are more religious than the majority population, with females tending to be more religious than males.

KEY POINT

Davie (1994) suggests that religious belief is important to ethnic minorities as a way of maintaining family, community and cultural identity in an alien or hostile environment. Johal (1998) notes that it functions to empower through difference when ethnic-minority religion comes into conflict with the increasingly secularised majority culture over issues such as worship in schools, the education of females, clothing requirements, etc. Bird argues that religion therefore functions to maintain cultural identity and resist assimilation in a mainly white and Christian society.

There is some evidence that religious belief may be declining among younger ethnic minorities. Johal (1998) notes that issues influenced by religion, such as diet and arranged marriages, may be negotiated with parents. Some British Asian youth may prefer to exert their 'Britishness' and adapt or reject these influences.

Hennels (1997) notes that many Afro-Caribbean people participate in the Pentecostal tradition which tends to subscribe to fundamentalist Christian values – e.g. encouraging hard work and a strict sexual and family morality. It may therefore attract members of the Afro-Caribbean minority who are experiencing economic, social and ethical deprivation. Marxists have been critical of Pentecostalism because they see its emphasis on religious experience as diverting Afro-Caribbean people from the real cause of their oppression, i.e. a racist capitalist system.

Rastafarianism has proved popular among young Afro-Caribbean men in the UK. There is some evidence that participation in this sect symbolises protest at the racial discrimination which young Afro-Caribbean men see as denying them full social and economic status.

Gender and religion

OCR U2533

An increasingly popular topic with examiners.

Women attend church more often and regularly than men. Walker (1990) argues that women are consequently more religious than men. Religion may be a way of compensating for a subordinate position in patriarchal societies. However, it may also be a function of age. Religious belief is more likely in middle and old age. There are more older women in the population than men.

KEY POINT

Almost all the major world religions are patriarchal and view women as subordinate and inferior. A number of religions see women's bodies and sexuality as threatening because menstruation and childbirth are seen to 'pollute' the spiritual purity of religious belief and places. Women are therefore policed by religion, e.g. there is widespread opposition in many religions to females conducting religious rituals.

Traditional ideas about women tend to characterise most fundamentalist religions. This is not surprising considering the fundamentalist desire to oppose modernity. However, it is important not to stereotype fundamentalist religions in terms of their attitudes towards women, e.g. it is often assumed that Islam is oppressive towards women, yet evidence from studies by Anwar and Butler suggests that Muslim women in the UK play an active rather than passive role in that religion.

Women do seem to play a greater role in NRMs and NAMs although some NRMs subscribe to what feminists would describe as oppressive beliefs about women. For example, the New Evangelical movements and groups such as Rastafarians and the Nation of Islam stress traditional roles for women in the home.

Bird suggests NAMs appeal to women more than men because their emphasis is on healing, co-operation, caring and spirituality (all regarded as feminine characteristics). Women may be more attracted to NAMs because they are more likely to experience social and psychic deprivation.

Progress check

1 According to Bryan Wilson, what has replaced religion in explaining the world?

2 What is disengagement?

3 What is religious pluralism?

4 Who argues that churches have to undergo secularisation before true religion can flourish?

5 Define religious fundamentalism.

6 Why might participation in Rastafarianism be symbolic for some Afro-Caribbeans?

7 How do most religions view women?

7 As inferior and subordinate.
6 Because it is a protest against racism.
5 It involves the belief that society needs to return to traditional ways of doing things, often these are defined by religious principles.
4 G.K. Nelson.
3 The fragmentation of monolithic religion into hundreds of religions competing with each other.
2 The withdrawal of the Church from important areas of social life, such as politics.
1 Scientific or rational thinking.

6.3 Religion and classical sociology

After studying this section you should be able to:

- *outline the relationship between religion, social control and social change*
- *describe the ideological function of religion*

Religion, stability and consensus: Functionalism

OCR ▶ U2533

Religion as an inhibitor of change for positive reasons.

Emile Durkheim believed that religion is central to the reproduction and maintenance of social order in societies. The major function of religion is to socialise society's members into value consensus by:

- **setting certain values apart** and infusing them with special significance. These values become '**moral codes**' or beliefs which society agrees to revere and socialise children into. Such codes formally and informally control our social behaviour,

- **encouraging collective worship**. Through worship the individual is encouraged to feel part of a wider moral community. Writers such as **Shils and Young** argue that today national ceremonies such as the funeral of Princess Diana perform a civil religion function in that they bring society together as a moral collective.

Later functionalist thinkers such as **Malinowski** see religious rites of passage as serving to help relieve the stress and anxieties created by life crises such as birth, puberty, marriage and death.

> Functionalists argue that the role of religion is to preserve the status quo rather than promote social change. Functionalists think that religion is a beneficial conservative force because it maintains consensus, integrates people into society and promotes social order.

KEY POINT

Criticism of functionalism identifies the following weaknesses.

- It is difficult to see how religion can be functioning to socialise the majority of society's members into morality and social integration if only a minority of people regularly attend church.

- There is little empirical evidence to support the view that national ceremonies such as the funeral of Diana result in social integration. It is merely assumed that they have that effect.

- Functionalists neglect the extent to which religion has been dysfunctional for society, e.g. in Northern Ireland religious divisions have caused social disruption and conflict rather than promoted social order.

It can be argued that Durkheim anticipated these criticisms by predicting that the rapid social change found in modern societies would result in a weakening of religious social controls.

Religion, ideology and conflict: Marxism

OCR   U2533

Like Durkheim, Marx also argued that religion was a conservative force in society. However, he did not agree that it is beneficial to society, arguing that the primary function of religion is to reproduce, maintain and legitimate class inequality, i.e. that:

- religion is an ideological apparatus which serves to reflect ruling-class ideas and interests.

- religion is the 'opium of the people' because it lulls the working class into a state of false class consciousness by making the true extent of their exploitation by the ruling class invisible.

Religion as an inhibitor of change for negative reasons.

> **KEY POINT**
>
> Religion was seen by Marx to be ideological in three ways:
>
> - It promotes the idea that the existing socio-economic hierarchy is God-given and therefore unchangeable.
>
> - Religion explains economic and social inequalities in supernatural terms. In other words, the real causes (i.e. exploitation by the ruling class) are obscured and distorted by religion's insistence that inequality is the product of sin or a sign that people have been chosen by God, etc.
>
> - Some religions even present suffering and poverty as a virtue to be welcomed and accepted as normal. Such ways of thinking promote the idea that there is no point in changing the here and now. Rather people should wait patiently for divine intervention.

Marx argued that religion functions to produce fatalistic followers uninterested in changing their physical world for the better.

There are a number of examples cited as evidence in favour of Marx's arguments:

- Halevy claims Methodism in the 19th century distracted workers from their class grievances and encouraged them to see enlightenment in terms of spirituality rather than revolution.

- Hook's analysis of the Catholic Church notes that it has a very conservative stance on contraception, abortion, women priests and homosexuality. Hook also suggests that the considerable wealth of the Catholic Church could be used to do more to tackle world poverty.

However, criticism of Marx has identified the following weaknesses:

- Like functionalism, Marxism fails to consider secularisation – the ideological power of religion is undermined by the fact that less than 10% of people attend church.

- There are examples of religious movements which have brought about radical social change. For example, the Reverend Martin Luther King and the Southern Baptist Church were important in dismantling segregation and bringing about political and social rights for black people in the USA in the 1960s. **Liberation theology**, (a combination of the teachings of Christ and Marx) has encouraged people to actively change society in Central America.

Religion as an promoter of change.

> **KEY POINT**
>
> **Engels** recognised that religion in some special circumstances could bring about radical change. He argued that ruling élites sometimes blocked all conventional avenues for change, e.g. politics, trade unions, etc., through force or ideology. Religion therefore, may be the only agency of change for some oppressed groups. The potential for change through religious avenues is enhanced by the presence of a charismatic leader who provides a focus for expressing discontent.

Religion, social action and social change: Weber

OCR ▷ U2533

Max Weber also subscribed to the idea that religion could be ideological in two ways:

- It gave assurance to the most fortunate, i.e. the powerful and wealthy, by stressing that their position was natural or God-given.
- It offered religious reasons for poverty and suffering in terms of themes such as wickedness, sins committed in former lives, etc. Weber argued, like Marx, that both these themes legitimate the status quo.

Religion as an promoter of change.

> **KEY POINT**
>
> Weber believed that some religious ideas, specifically Protestant beliefs, had initiated the economic and social conditions in which capitalism emerged. From his comparative studies, Weber noted that while similar economic conditions prevailed in China, India and Europe, capitalism only developed in the latter. He noted that capitalism had developed in those parts of Europe where a particular set of Protestant beliefs known as **Calvinism** were dominant. He concluded that Calvinism had brought about the right cultural climate for capitalist ideas and practices to develop in two ways:

- Calvinists believed in **predestination**, i.e. that they were chosen by God for salvation. They were taught to believe that righteous living was all-important and that their reward for sticking to such religious principles would be economic success.

> **KEY POINT**
>
> - Calvinism encouraged values such as self-discipline, hard work, thrift, modesty and the rejection of self-indulgence, pleasure, idleness and lavish spending: the 'Protestant Work Ethic'. The adoption of these ideas, Weber argues, led to the rapid accumulation of capital and the emergence of a Calvinist capitalist class at the end of the feudal era.

Don't make the mistake of using the word 'cause'.

Weber did not say Calvinism 'caused' capitalism, he only suggested that it was the major contributor to a climate of change. Many other pre-conditions needed to be in place, e.g. Calvinist beliefs had to be supplemented by a certain level of technology, a skilled and mobile workforce and rational modes of law and bureaucracy. These latter pre-conditions were also present in China and India but Weber claimed that Eastern religions emphasised the spiritual rather than the rational or material, i.e. ideas not conducive to sustained economic activity.

Criticism of Weber has included the following points:

- **Sombart** suggests that Weber was mistaken about the beliefs held by Calvinists – Calvinism was against greed and the pursuit of money for its own sake.

- Some countries with large Calvinist populations did not industrialise, which is cited as evidence that Weber's thesis is wrong. However, **Marshall** points out that Weber did not claim that Calvinism was the *sole* pre-condition for the emergence of capitalism, for example, Scotland lacked a skilled technical labour force and capital for investment.

- Some commentators have suggested that slavery, colonialism and piracy generated a super-accumulation of capital and that this was more influential in the emergence of capitalism in the West than Calvinist beliefs.

- Marxists have also been critical of Weber. **Kautsky** suggested that capitalism pre-dated Calvinism. Bourgeoise capitalists were attracted to it because it offered convenient justification for the pursuit of economic interests – the Protestant religion was an **ideology** used to legitimate capitalist interests.

Despite some empirical difficulties in testing Weber's thesis, his ideas remain important because he highlighted the relationship between **social structure** (i.e. the economic and social system) and **social action** (i.e. interaction and interpretation). His point was that if certain structural factors are present, people may **choose** to act upon religious ideas and bring about change.

Progress check

1 What are moral codes?

2 What does dysfunctional mean?

3 What is an ideology?

4 What is the role of religious ideology according to Marxists?

5 What does Engels argue?

6 What Protestant religion helped to bring about capitalism according to Weber?

7 What was the Protestant Work Ethic?

7 A set of ideas subscribed to by Calvinists which stress hard work, idleness as a sin, thrift, etc.
6 Calvinism.
5 That under certain circumstances, religion can bring about revolutionary change.
4 To reproduce, maintain and legitimate class inequality. To prevent social change.
3 A set of powerful ideas used to justify some type of inequality.
2 Harmful, problematic.
1 Values that society reveres and sets apart as sacred and all-important.

Sample question and model answer

A typical OCR question.

a) Identify and illustrate two features of secularisation. [20 marks]

15 minutes on part a).

a) Wilson argues that secularisation is the process by which religious institutions and practices lose their social significance. He suggests that this is reflected statistically in declining church attendance and membership. For example, there has been an overall decline of approximately 25% in membership of the established churches since 1970. Wilson also argues that we can measure secularisation by looking at how religious institutions like the Roman Catholic and Anglican Churches have declined in political power since the middle ages. Wilson argues that the near unity of the church and the state has undergone disengagement or separation. Consequently, the church now exercises little influence over government.

30 minutes on part b).

b) Outline and assess the view that religious movements act as a conservative influence on modern society. [40 marks]

b) Sociologists generally view institutions like the Church of England and the Catholic Church as exercising a conservative influence over society in a number of ways. First, churches generally do not tolerate any challenge to their religious truth and authority. Second, some churches, notably the Catholic Church, have conservative stances on homosexuality, contraception, sex before marriage, women priests, etc.

Functionalists such as Durkheim and Parsons suggest that such conservatism has a positive function to play in society in that churches and denominations provide guidelines for human actions and standards against which people's conduct can be judged. In this sense, religion contributes to a value consensus which functionalists see as necessary for social order in society.

Assessment implied by contrasting theories.

Marxists also argue that the role of institutional religion is essentially conservative. Marx described religion as 'the opium of the people' because, like the drug, it functioned to dull people's senses to class inequality and exploitation. It did this by promising, for example, eternal life in heaven in return for suffering and poverty here and now on Earth. He also claimed churches serve the dominant class by justifying their power and consequently social inequality. There is no doubt that church movements are ideologically conservative. An opinion poll in 1988 found that a majority of active lay members of the Church of England supported the Conservative party, whilst the bishopry is recruited from a very narrow upper-class public-school and Oxbridge-educated base. Feminists have been critical of the conservative attitudes demonstrated by institutional religion towards women.

Assess.

However, there is also evidence that religion has promoted social change in some societies by acting as the focus of opposition. In Poland, the Roman Catholic Church opposed the communist government and in Latin America liberation theology has encouraged revolution in Nicaragua (although priests subscribing to this view have been expelled from the Church).

Sects can be seen to be conservative because they place severe restrictions on their member's behaviour. For example, they often act as total institutions controlling all aspects of members' behaviour. They are often puritanical. Furthermore, they sometimes suggest that poverty and inequality is caused by sin and will only be solved in an after-life. In this sense, sects can be seen to be ideological because they do not encourage people to change their situation here and now.

Practice examination questions

1 Identify and explain two ways in which religion may socially control the behaviour of women. [20 marks]

2 Outline and assess the view that religion has become disengaged from society. [40 marks]

Chapter 7

Youth and culture

The following topics are covered in this chapter:

- *Youth and youth sub-cultures*
- *Youth and deviance*

7.1 Youth and youth sub-cultures

After studying this section you should be able to:

- *distinguish between youth sub-culture and deviant youth sub-cultures*
- *identify the differences between functionalist, Marxist and post-modernist theories of youth sub-culture*

LEARNING SUMMARY

Theories of youth culture

OCR ▷ U2533

Pearson (1983) points out that adolescents have consistently been defined as a problem since the 19th century. However, youth defined as a separate social category from children and adults only became the subject of sociological and media interest in the 1950s. Early theories focused on the concept of youth culture, i.e. the idea that young people in general shared a common culture and identity which set them apart from adults.

Early sociological attempts to explain why youth cultures had emerged focused on three potential causes:

- Abrams (1959) argued that youth cultures were caused by 'affluence without responsibility' – young people had too much money to spend and too few responsibilities. Manufacturers responded by setting up a specifically teenage leisure industry revolving around fashion and music.

- Secondary education was expanded in 1944. This allegedly led to large numbers of young people in schools seeing themselves as 'different' to adult society.

- The mass media were seen as responsible for the rapid dissemination of youth-culture styles.

The functionalist theory

OCR ▷ U2533

> The functionalist sociologist, Eisenstadt (1956) argued that the general function of youth cultures is to smooth the **transition** between childhood and adulthood. He argued that adolescents generally experience status contradictions and powerlessness within the family, and therefore lack a stable identity and status. As a result, they turn to their peers for support. In this way, youth cultures are **functional** to society because they ease the tricky transition from childhood to adulthood and maintain social order.
>
> **KEY POINT**

Eisenstadt's analysis was criticised in three ways:

- He implies that the transition from youth to adulthood is a universal experience. However, not all young people experience this transition in the same way.

- He implied that youth is homogeneous, and thus ignored social class, gender and ethnic divisions between young people, i.e. some people are more marginalised and powerless than others.

- He attempted to explain the generation gap that had supposedly opened up between teenagers and adults. However, a number of surveys have questioned the existence of such a gap, e.g. research by **Wyn and White (1997)** found 'most young people tend to be fairly conventional in outlook and lifestyle', whilst **Balding (1995)** found that three-quarters of 16-year-olds turned to their parents when they had a problem.

The Marxist theory

OCR ▸ U2S33

During the 1970s and early 1980s, most sociological attention was paid to the concept of **deviant youth 'sub-cultures'** – the idea that some young people belonged to groups with their own norms, values, rituals, sanctions and dress codes which were antagonistic to mainstream culture. Over the past fifty years, youth groups such as teddy-boys (1950s), mods and rockers (1960s), skinheads (late 1960s), punks (1970s) and ravers (1980s) have all attracted sociological study because they seem to stand apart from conventional society with their distinctive, seemingly organised and sometimes illegal lifestyles.

In the 1970s, the question of **class divisions** within youth cultures was examined by Marxist writers especially those associated with the **Centre for Contemporary Cultural Studies (CCCS)**. Generally, sociologists associated with this approach have linked the development of youth sub-cultures to **changes in the economic structure of society**.

> **KEY POINT**
>
> It was argued by sociologists such as **Cohen (1972)**, **Hall and Jefferson (1976)** and **Clarke** that it was important to study the meaning of sub-cultural style for young people because:
> - such styles reflected the declining social and economic circumstances of working-class youth in inner cities
> - specifically working-class youth cultures were seen as an attempt to **symbolically** or **'magically'** re-create traditional notions of working-class community through dress, style and behaviour
> - such styles represented a form of working-class ideological or cultural resistance to ruling class/bourgeois **hegemony** .

Hegemony = cultural dominance of ruling class.

Mods

Hedonism = living for pleasure.

Cohen (1972) argued that mod sub-cultures in the 1960s were a symbolic attempt to achieve the status denied to them by their low status and dead-end jobs. Their obsession with a hedonist lifestyle (through the acquisition of the latest fashions, motor scooters, dancing and drugs) was a means of expressing that status. It also symbolised their rejection of the mundane existence allocated to them by capitalism.

Skinheads

Cohen and Clarke argued that skinhead gangs in the early 1970s were an exaggerated attempt to recreate traditional notions of working-class community – communities in decline because of recession and slum clearance. Skinheads blamed outsiders (such as immigrants) for this decline and attempted to reassert working-class culture through their value system, dress and behaviour. They also:

- organised themselves collectively in gangs which emphasised loyalty, toughness and masculinity
- defended territory aggressively from rival gangs
- targeted groups they saw as their ideological enemies with extreme violence, e.g. immigrants, students and homosexuals

- borrowed style elements from working-class occupations (e.g. the Doc Marten industrial boots, braces, haircut, etc). This very aggressive look was meant to strike fear into mainstream society and to symbolise their resistance to establishment institutions such as the educational system and the police.

In this context, sub-cultural style represents an attempt to assert power by those denied it through conventional channels.

Punk rock

Dick Hebdige's 'Subculture – The Meaning of Style' focused on punk rock which emerged in the late 1970s. Hebdige argued that punk was a form of resistance to a society considered by youth to be in social, moral and economic decline. Punk style took conventional items such as safety pins, razor blades, etc. and shocked mainstream society by wearing them as fashion accessories. Punk rock was thus a critique of a society that punks saw as conformist and lacking in imagination. However, Hebdige notes that punk sub-culture was short-lived.

> The explanation for this Hebdidge termed incorporation – big business and the media quickly learn to exploit youth sub-cultural styles for profit in two ways:
>
> - through 'commodity incorporation' – elements of youth style are transformed into youth commodities which are marketed and sold as fashion accessories, e.g. punk style (in particular, ripped t-shirts, razor-blade ear-rings, hair gel, etc.) was quickly commercialised
> - through ideological incorporation which trivialises sub-cultural styles, e.g. articles in the media about punks concluded that they were confused youngsters going through a phase. As Abbott (1999) argues 'punk came to be labelled as exotic and spirited, perhaps even funny, but also quite harmless'.

KEY POINT

Critique of the Marxist view

The explanations for sub-cultures produced by Marxists can be criticised on the following grounds:

- Subcultural styles persisted long after the economic and social changes described in the CCCS analysis.
- Why do very different responses emerge if structural changes are the most important variable? It doesn't account for the adoption of some of these styles by middle-class youth.
- There is no empirical evidence that youth interpret their styles in the same way as the CCCS do. There is also a danger that such sociologists read too much into these styles or see what they want to see.
- Only a very small minority of youth have ever been involved in deviant sub-cultures. The majority of young people lead very mundane and conformist lives.
- The CCCS neglected race (although black youth in general is an under-researched area). However, Hebdige points out that black culture and music have heavily influenced most white sub-cultures.

Moral panic theory

OCR　▷　U2533

Note that this material is relevant to the representation of age in Chapter 5.

Stan Cohen argues that many deviant youth sub-cultures are effectively created, maintained and killed-off by the mass media. Youth cultures are not coherent social groupings that appear spontaneously as a reaction to structural forces such as class.

It is likely that youth sub-cultures did not exist outside of a small core of devotees. Cohen asserts that the media labelled or stereotyped youth groups by sensationalising stories about them, so creating something out of nothing. These **moral panics** grossly exaggerated the threat posed by these groups and this led to their 'demonisation', i.e. the creation of **folk devils**. Youth cultures were then seen as a problem that the government, police and courts needed to stamp out.

A classic recent example of this is the **acid house** movement – groups of people with nothing in common except a desire to party – manufactured by the media into a defined youth sub-culture with common interests, aims and beliefs.

Youth and gender

OCR　▷　U2533

McRobbie and Garber (1976) are critical of the CCCS analysis because it failed to explain how the masculine culture of many deviant sub-cultures impacted negatively on the lives of females. They argue that the nature of male youth culture has meant boys have been able to control public spaces such as the street-corner and that consequently females were confined to traditional areas such as the home (and, in particular, their bedrooms).

This material is also relevant to gender identity found in Chapter 4.

> **KEY POINT**
>
> **McRobbie and Garber** argue that girls subscribe to a 'bedroom culture' which places a high value on passive femininity and which revolves around reading romantic magazines and thinking and talking about boys with their female friends. It also allows girls to express sexual yearnings in a relatively safe way. Sexual fantasies about pop stars, for example, allow the expression of a girls sexuality in ways that don't threaten her reputation. If girls do rebel, it is expressed by acting in a male way – acquiring a sexual reputation (whether deserved or not), by hanging around boys, or by getting pregnant.

According to **Abbott and Wallace (1990)** the behaviour of teenage girls is partly an outcome of their socialisation into family ideology. In particular, girls were much more likely than boys to have their movements outside the home controlled by parents. Recent studies have indicated that jobs are probably more important for young women than membership of a youth culture because these bring about status and economic independence. **Lees** notes that young working-class girls were less likely to prioritise love, marriage and children in the 1990s. Careers were viewed by Lees' sample as their major goal.

However, such aspirations are still negatively influenced by factors such as the male dominance of public space and sexuality, the ideology of marriage and motherhood, and the patriarchal assumptions that underpin the labour market. All these factors may combine to disadvantage young females.

Youth culture in the 1980s and 1990s

OCR　▷　U2533

In the 1980s there appeared to be a fragmentation of youth culture. Very few cultural patterns of the period, e.g. goths, new romantics, etc. seemed to have the same cultural power in terms of the shock or resistance value of skinheads, punks, etc.

McRobbie (1994) has focused on the impact of changes in the social and economic position of young women. She argues that young women are increasingly reclaiming public space, e.g. she notes that black 'ragga girls' use sexually explicit dancing in order to ridicule male sexism and re-assert female control over sexuality.

KEY POINT

A good example of both a recent youth culture and moral panic.

Redhead (1990) questions Willis' assertion that oppositional youth sub-cultures are a thing of the past. His work on rave culture suggests that it contained elements which were symbolic of resistance to both the establishment and mainstream culture. It can be argued that the media moral panic about rave culture's use of ecstasy and the subsequent State and police crackdown indicates the existence of a genuine counter-culture.

Post-modernism and youth sub-cultures

OCR U2533

Post-modernists note how cultural industries remove youth styles from their original contexts, rob them of their cultural and political meaning and turn them into superficial fashion statements.

Hebdige argues that new technologies such as the Internet allow youth the opportunity to circumvent the media and cultural industries' dominance of how they should express themselves. It has facilitated virtual or proto youth cultures which require no collective physical interaction and which may reduce the importance of class, gender and ethnicity. However, **Osgerby (1998)** argues that the commercial youth market may be in decline because the fashion, music and film industries are more interested in targeting the more affluent 'thirty-something' generation.

This material brings the sociology of youth up to date.

Reimer (1995) argues that the central feature of youth in modern societies is the preoccupation with 'fun' – the constant search for excitement that cuts across all other sources of identity (class, gender, ethnicity, etc.). Greater emphasis, therefore, is now being placed on attempts to explain the 'ordinariness' of modern youth. Recent surveys, such as the 2020 Vision research (1997), show that youth is committed to family life, work, education and anti-crime attitudes in much the same way as their parents.

KEY POINT

Taylor *et al.* suggest a 'new' sociology of youth has emerged which sees the study of youth leisure styles as being less relevant than problems such as homelessness, rising suicide rates, unemployment, low income, drugs, and social marginalisation. **Walker (1996)** and **Wilkinson (1996)**, for example, are concerned about political apathy amongst the young.

Progress check

1 Identify three influences on the emergence of youth cultures in the 1950s.

2 Who argued that the function of youth cultures is to ease the transition from childhood to adulthood?

3 How do working-class sub-cultures resist ruling-class culture?

4 What does hegemony mean?

5 What is the cause of youth culture according to Stan Cohen?

6 What is a proto youth culture?

7 What is the 'new' sociology of youth?

7 One which focuses on social problems such as suicide.
6 One in which people do not physically meet but have common interests through a lifestyle interest such as the Internet.
5 Mass-media moral panics.
4 Cultural dominance of the ruling class.
3 Through adopting a style which magically creates working-class culture and shocks convention.
2 Eisenstadt.
1 Affluence, education and mass media.

7.2 Youth and deviance

After studying this section you should be able to:

- *identify patterns and trends in delinquency according to social class, gender and ethnicity*
- *outline and assess functionalist, Marxist and feminist accounts of delinquent sub-cultures.*

LEARNING SUMMARY

Theories of juvenile delinquency

OCR ▷ U2533

Official statistics show that juvenile crime has declined in recent years after having reached a peak in 1984–85. Ricky Taylor's (1998) analysis of official statistics between 1957 and 1997 shows that in 1958, 56% of all offenders found guilty or cautioned were aged 20 or under. In 1997, the proportion was 38%. However, only one in ten crimes result in arrest and conviction so it is likely that youth involvement in crime is higher than official statistics indicate.

Sub-cultural theories

Over the past fifty years, a number of sociological studies have focused on juvenile delinquency. A.K. Cohen's study of American delinquency argues that working-class boys commit crime for two reasons:

- their parents fail to equip them with the right skills required for success in education
- like all members of society, they require status, school denies them status, and out of frustration they form anti-school sub-cultures (counter-cultures), which award status for deviant activities.

> Paul Willis' study suggests working-class lads define status in different ways to teachers and academic boys.

Walter Miller argued that working-class youth gets into trouble because they exaggerate the values of their parents' working-class culture in order to give meaning to their lives, i.e. in order to compensate for the boredom of school and factory work. Such youth therefore subscribes to a sub-culture made up of values which revolve around **masculinity** – especially drinking, being tough and seeing violence as an acceptable means of solving problems, wanting excitement, risk-taking behaviour, and fatalism. Commitment to such values brings them into contact with the police, etc. However, this theory has been accused of **ethnocentrism** because it stereotypes the working class and implies that middle-class culture is somehow superior.

Labelling theory

> Think about how such processes affect identity (see Chapter 4).

Labelling theory argues that powerful groups shape social attitudes to deviance by making the rules for powerless groups such as the young. Consequently young people are **labelled** via policing or media moral panics. Studies of policing in both Britain (Smith and Grey, Holdaway) and USA (Cicourel) suggest young people, especially young blacks, are negatively labelled as either suspicious or criminal in everyday policing – which results in over-proportionate stops and arrests. Matza argues that most people subscribe to some deviant values, not just working-class youth. He calls these **subterranean values**, but working-class youth is more likely to be negatively labelled than others for the same behaviour.

> **KEY POINT**
>
> This theory suggests that once labelled as being deviant, the deviant status becomes a **master status** which has negative consequences – once labelled, young people may see themselves as deviant. Youth sub-cultures are then viewed positively by their members because they confer normality and status on those labelled negatively by society and may compensate for the negative societal reaction.

Marxist theory

The Marxists, **Taylor, Walton and Young** argue that capitalist society is characterised by great inequalities in wealth and power (i.e. class inequality). Working-class youth commit crime because of their experience of these injustices. **Gilroy** argues that black street crime is political, reflecting young black people's anger at the way that white society has historically treated black people via slavery and colonialism. It is a rational response to contemporary discrimination, especially police harassment.

Left Realism

An extremely important theory – know it well! Marginalisation = lack of power and status.

> **KEY POINT**
>
> The Left Realists, **Lea and Young**, point out that working-class crime committed by young people in the inner cities is 'wearing down' working-class communities (indicated by victim surveys). This theory argues that working-class and black youth turn to street crime because of relative deprivation. In comparison with their peers (i.e. middle-class and white youth) they feel deprived in terms of education, jobs, income, standard of living, etc. and they feel they are powerless to change their situation. They may feel that nobody listens to them or that they are picked on, e.g. police harassment, and therefore may turn to sub-cultures – these may be positive and offer status through legitimate and conventional means (e.g. a church group) or negative in that status is awarded for deviant behaviour, including crime.

Conservative control criminology

Also a very important theory.

The Conservative Criminologist, **Hirschi**, argues that much criminality is opportunistic. People choose to commit crime because the benefits often outweigh the risks and costs (i.e. getting caught and punished). Older people do not commit crime because they usually have controls in their lives which mean that the costs of crime far outweigh the benefits of crime. Such controls include attachment to family (e.g. marriage and children), commitment to a career, active involvement in a community and reputation. The young are less likely to have such controls in their lives and the benefits of crime clearly outweigh the risks of being caught and punished.

Feminity, masculinity and youth crime

OCR   U2533

Feminism

Feminists note that young women are less likely than young men to appear in the criminal statistics. This may partly be due to women being less likely to be stopped, arrested and charged by the police compared with men. Female youth is much more likely to be cautioned than male youth. However, the statistics have shown a rise in female violence recently – especially gang violence.

Note that this material is relevant to the debate about gender identity in Chapter 4.

Feminists suggest that the differences between the sexes in terms of criminality can be attributed to different socialisation during childhood and adolescence. Male teenagers may experiment with 'masculine' values which revolve around risk-taking behaviour, toughness, aggression, proving oneself, etc. and the pursuit of these may lead to conflicts with authority. The value system of girls stresses domestic responsibilities and passivity. Smart, in her study of female and male delinquency, found that girls are more strictly supervised by their parents and have less opportunity to engage in juvenile delinquency. Shacklady-Smith's (1978) study of female delinquents discovered that they had been labelled by parents and teachers as 'unfeminine'. Once labelled, they responded with aggressive behaviour, became more dependent upon a delinquent sub-culture and turned to more extreme types of delinquency.

Girl gangs

There is some concern that violent crimes committed by young working-class women are rising. Studies of girl gangs in the USA by Campbell and Nicoll note that violence, drug dealing, robbery and possession of dangerous weapons are common activities carried out by young women. These women joined gangs to compensate for low status in their families and communities and as an alternative to taking on low-skilled, tedious, low-paid jobs. Gangs were seen to offer security, companionship and protection. However, such gangs did contain elements of traditional patriarchal culture – female gangs were regarded as auxiliaries to the male gangs. Campbell notes that many of the women were girlfriends of male gang members. Many became pregnant and moved uncomplainingly into traditional mother roles. Nicoll suggests girl gangs are increasing in the UK, although she says they seem less organised and violent.

The crisis of masculinity

Recent research by feminists and sociologists such as Mac En Ghaill has started to examine the way masculinity is constructed in modern societies. Mac En Ghaill suggests that the workforce is becoming more feminised and job opportunities for young men are declining. Young males may thus be experiencing a 'crisis of masculinity', i.e. their traditional roles are disappearing. It is argued that this is creating anxiety which may only be resolved by joining anti-school sub-cultures or by involvement in violence and crime. Such activities may be a way of re-affirming masculinity.

Progress check

1 What is a counter-culture?

2 What is relative deprivation?

3 Who argues that juvenile delinquency is caused by the benefits of crime outweighing the costs of crime?

4 Which social group is most likely to be cautioned?

4 Female adolescents.
3 Hirschi, the Conservative Criminologist.
2 The feeling that you are deprived compared with another similar group.
1 An anti-school culture.

Sample question and model answer

A typical OCR question.

15 minutes on part a).

a) Identify and explain two ways in which youth cultures may function to ease the transition from childhood to adulthood. **[20 marks]**

a) This is mainly a functionalist argument associated with Eisenstadt. He argued that peer groups, in contrast with the meritocratic education system, offer a relaxed world in which people are valued for who they are rather than how well they performed. Membership of a peer group also helps manage and negotiate independence from the family group.

30 minutes on part b).

b) Outline and assess the view that working-class sub-cultural styles symbolise a form of resistance to ruling-class culture. **[40 marks]**

Outline the argument, i.e. Marxist.

b) This idea is mainly associated with the Centre for Contemporary Cultural Studies (CCCS). Sociologists associated with this approach suggest that it is important to study the meaning of sub-cultural style for young people. Such styles also represented a form of working-class ideological or cultural resistance to bourgeois cultural dominance.

For example, Cohen and Clarke argued that skinhead gangs were an exaggerated attempt to 'magically' recreate traditional notions of working-class community. Such communities were in decline because of recession in traditional working-class industries and slum clearance.

However, skinheads blamed outsiders such as immigrants for this decline. The response of skinhead youth was to stress traditional elements of working-class culture through their value system, dress and behaviour. Their style borrowed elements from working-class work (e.g. the Doc Marten industrial boots, braces, the haircut, etc.). This very aggressive look was meant to strike fear into mainstream society and to symbolise their resistance to establishment institutions such as the educational system and the police.

A later study in this vein was Dick Hebdige's 'Subculture – The Meaning of Style' which focused on punk rock which emerged in the late 1970s. Hebdige argues that punk style took conventional items such as safety pins and razor blades and deliberately used them to shock mainstream society. For example, safety pins were worn through the nose. National symbols such as the union jack and pictures of the Queen were used in ways intended to outrage. For example, the cover of the single 'God Save the Queen' showed her with a safety pin through her nose. According to Hebdige, punk rock was a critique of a society that punks saw as conformist and lacking in any imagination.

Assess.

However, Hebdige notes such resistance is shortlived because the media neutralise the symbolic resistance of youth sub-cultural style. Youth commodities are marketed and sold as fashion accessories. For example, Hebdige notes that punk style, e.g. ripped t-shirts, razor-blade ear-rings, hair gel, etc. was quickly commercialised. Secondly, articles in the media about punks concluded that they were confused youngsters going through a phase.

However, the CCCS account has been criticised because it failed to explain why some youth chose specific styles rather than others. It also fails to account for why the majority of working-class youth do not get involved with such deviant cultures. There is no empirical evidence that youth interpret their styles in the way the CCCS envisage. There is also a

Sample question and model answer (continued)

More assessment.

danger that such sociologists are reading too much into these styles or seeing what they want to see. Stan Cohen argues that many deviant youth sub-cultures were probably socially constructed by the media. It is likely that these youth sub-cultures did not exist outside of a small core of devotees. The CCCS school has also been accused of neglecting working-class girls and blacks in its analysis.

Practice examination questions

1 Identify and explain two reasons why deviant sub-cultures might appear in schools.

[20 marks]

2 Outline and assess the different ways in which sociologists have used the concept of sub-culture to explain juvenile crime.

[40 marks]

Chapter 8

Wealth, welfare and poverty

The following topics are covered in this chapter:

- **Wealth and poverty**
- **Welfare**

8.1 Wealth and poverty

After studying this section you should be able to:

- outline different definitions of poverty, wealth and income
- assess different explanations of the distribution of poverty, wealth and income between different social groups
- explain the existence and persistence of poverty

LEARNING SUMMARY

The distribution of income and wealth

AQA   U2

Always be on the look out for more up-to-date statistics.

A number of observations can be made about the distribution of income between 1945–97.

- Income inequality generally narrowed between 1945 and 1979 because of full employment and the Welfare State. However, this should not be exaggerated.

- Between 1979–97 income inequality widened until it was at its most unequal since records began at the end of the 19th century. This was due to the top rate of income tax being lowered, an increase in VAT from 8% to 17½% and large salary rises for business leaders.

- In 1991 women's average weekly pay was 71% of the male average wage but in 1997 the gap widened for the first time in ten years.

- There were large regional variations in average incomes from employment and other sources. The highest paid region was the South East. There was not really a North–South divide as much as London/South East–Rest divide.

- The average earnings of 18–20 year olds fell from 61% to 53% of overall average earnings in 1996.

Changes in wealth distribution

Overall the 20th century has seen a gradual redistribution of wealth in the UK – e.g. in 1911 the richest 1% of the population owned 69% of wealth but this had fallen to 18% by 1991. However, redistribution has been very narrow – from the very wealthy (the top 1%) to the wealthy (the top 10%), i.e. family members in order to avoid paying death duties.

Rich lists are published quite often by newspapers although you need to be aware of their limitations.

Inheritance is still an important source of wealth. Harbury and Hitchens (1979) found that 36% of those in the top 0.1% of wealthy had inherited their wealth in 1973. The *Sunday Times* 'Rich List' of 1999 indicated that 291 of the 1000 featured on the list had inherited their wealth.

One form of wealth that increased in the 1980s was the ownership of company shares. By 1988, 21% of people owned shares because of the privatisation of public utilities in this period (e.g. British Telecom). However, John Scott points out the richest 1% of the population own 75% of all privately owned shares. The distribution of shares has actually narrowed in the 1990s as those who bought shares for the first time in the 1980s have now sold them.

However, knowledge about the distribution of wealth is vague because:

- inland revenue statistics depend on income and wealth declared. The wealthy have methods (e.g. overseas tax havens, etc.) which mean that only a fraction of their wealth and income becomes known to the authorities;

- wealth statistics tend to be based on death duties, but the wealthy transfer assets to other family members before death to avoid such duties;

- even a great deal of the *Sunday Times* list is speculation rather than hard fact.

These problems mean that wealth is likely to be underestimated rather than overestimated.

Definitions of poverty

AQA ▶ U2

> Marshall (1999) defines poverty as a state in which resources, usually material, but sometimes cultural, are lacking.
>
> **KEY POINT**

Absolute or subsistence poverty

> This describes the state in which people lack the minimum resources required for survival. They lack the basic opportunities of material well-being needed for 'health and working efficiency'. This definition assumes that it is possible to set a poverty benchmark below which no one should fall.
>
> **KEY POINT**

Absolute definitions of poverty are often compared and contrasted with relative definitions of poverty.

Seebohm Rowntree's (1899) study of poverty in York in the late 19th century involved a minimum standard of living required for basic survival. Rowntree worked out a minimum diet, clothing and shelter needed by a family. In 1899, Rowntree found that 15% of York's population were living in primary poverty – i.e. they had insufficient earnings to meet even their most basic needs. When he repeated this study in 1936 and 1950 he found that this figure had fallen to approximately 7% and 3%, respectively.

The level of income support paid to an individual or family is based on what the government believes it is reasonably possible to live on. Therefore the number of people who claim or who are eligible to claim income support can be said to be 'officially' in poverty prior to claiming.

The strengths of the absolute model of poverty are that:

- as a definition, it is clear and unambiguous. It is not confused by degrees of poverty. It states very simply that if people lack specific resources, they are poor

- as Cole (1999) notes, it is useful for making historical and international comparisons because basic physical needs are similar in most societies

- it has a moral and emotive impact. 'Absolute' stresses the minimum required for survival. Most people would therefore agree that something needs to be done about it.

The weaknesses of the absolute model of poverty are that:

- it focuses on physical needs and does not pay enough attention to social and psychological needs, e.g. basic needs might include the right to education and/or literacy, easy access to health care, a safe environment, etc.

The weaknesses of this definition tend to be the strengths of the relative definition.

- the living standards of a particular society tend to rise over time. Consequently, people's expectations in regards to 'needs' also change over time. In Britain, over the course of the 20th century, luxuries have become comforts and comforts have become necessities. Similarly, social expectations about life expectancy have changed too – access to better quality health care means that people expect to live longer

- as Cole (1999) argues, absolutist definitions fail to consider that the poor may lack the knowledge or resources to use what they have effectively, e.g. they may be unaware of what constitutes nutritional foods. They may lack the material advantages enjoyed by other sections of society which allow them to buy more cheaply and in bulk, e.g. access to a car, freezers, etc.

- definitions of absolute poverty involve subjective judgements about what 'health' actually is and how to maintain it. The numbers in 'poverty' can be increased or decreased by moving the poverty line.

Relative poverty models

AQA   U2

> **KEY POINT**
>
> **Peter Townsend (1979)** defined relative poverty as lacking the resources to enjoy the living conditions, amenities and rituals that the mass of society take for granted. Townsend sees resources as including income, housing, education, health and other social services. Using this definition, poverty exists when the individual's standard of living is significantly lower than that of other people according to the conventions of the day. In other words, definitions of poverty are not fixed – they reflect constantly changing living standards and therefore changing cultural expectations. Poverty therefore is specific to societies, and even to sub-cultures, age-groups, regions, etc. within those societies.

Townsend's (1979) survey asked questions about 60 indicators of deprivation relating to family access to diet, housing, amenities, etc. He then constructed a 'deprivation index' of 12 indicators of lifestyle including not having a fridge, not having sole use of a bathroom, not having a week's holiday away from home over the previous year and children not having a party on their last birthday. Townsend concluded that over 40 of his 60 indicators indicated a strong relationship between deprivation and income. He thus determined the point when lack of resources leads to a qualitative decline in living standards compared with the rest of the population. He set this 40% above the government's 'supplementary benefit' level. Using this relative measurement he concluded that 22.9% of the population were living in poverty.

Social consensus poverty model

A variation on Townsend's approach was the social consensus approach of the Breadline Britain surveys carried out by Joanna Mack and Stewart Lansley in 1983 and 1990.

Mack and Lansley asked a representative sample of ordinary people what they felt were 'necessities'. People were defined as living in poverty if they could not afford three or more necessities. On this basis, Mack and Lansley concluded that one in seven of the population was living in poverty in 1983. The number in poverty increased to one in five of the population in 1990. They concluded that these findings showed that society generally shared similar meanings in regard to necessities.

The relativist approach has two main strengths:

- The approach reveals changes in both the standard of living of a society and its cultural expectations. Consequently sociologists are able to chart the evolution of deprivation and governments can therefore respond with social policy, e.g. by raising benefit levels.

- Consensus definitions are by no means perfect and are still to some degree socially constructed. For example, media representations of both affluence and poverty may impact on people's perceptions and definitions of necessities. However, they may be more reliable than studies which rely on the subjective interpretation of individual sociologists.

The weaknesses of the Relative/Consensus Models are as follows:

- It is fairly easy to identify social necessities, but not so easy to say precisely how these relate to levels of income, expenditure and consumption. Lack of necessities may be due to a shortage of income but the shortage of income itself might be caused by lack of consumer knowledge about prices, etc.

- If poverty is defined in terms of income-support rates, a government decision to increase the real value of benefits will simultaneously increase the numbers deemed to be living in 'poverty'.

> The weaknesses of this definition tend to be the strengths of the relative definition.

> **KEY POINT**
>
> The Joseph Rowntree Foundation's Inquiry into Income and Wealth (1995) defined the poor as those living on less than 50% of average income. On the basis of this definition in 1993, it calculated 25% of the population were living in poverty compared with 9% in 1979. Changes in taxation, the increase in lone parents, falls in the real value of benefits, and increased unemployment had contributed to a growth in inequality and poverty.

An Essex University study 'Changing Places' (1996), found that for families who managed to escape poverty this was very often a temporary respite – 41% of their sample who escaped poverty slipped back into poverty during the course of their research.

Progress check

1 What happened to income inequality between 1979–97?

2 What has been the main direction of the redistribution of wealth?

3 What did Rowntree discover about poverty in York between 1899–1936?

4 What percentage of the population were living in poverty according to (a) Townsend, (b) Mack and Lansley and (c) the Joseph Rowntree Trust?

4 (a) 23% (b) 20% (c) 25%.
3 Absolute poverty fell from 15% of the population to 3%.
2 From the extremely wealthy (top 1%) to the very wealthy (top 10%).
1 It was at its most unequal since records began.

The social distribution of poverty

AQA   U2

These statistics are often updated by newspapers and government. Keep a look-out for more recent figures!

The following groups have been consistently poor since Rowntree's day.

- **The elderly.** A third of all pensioners were claiming means-tested benefits to supplement their pension in 1994. 15% were claiming income support, and it is estimated that one million do not claim what they are entitled to.

- **The sick and disabled.** In 1998, 34% of all people with disabilities were living in poverty. Over 50% of the disabled are of pensionable age.

- **Single parents.** There are 1.3 million lone parents in the UK. Just under one million claim income support.

- **Children.** Middleton *et al.*, (1997) survey of 1,239 children, 'Small Fortunes' concluded that one in ten children are poor and that the children of single parents are worst affected.

- **The unemployed.** In February 1998, there were officially 1.85 million unemployed according to official figures – although with the inclusion of women and young people on training programmes, it could be as high as 4.24 million. Some groups, e.g. the low skilled, the young and ethnic minorities, are more likely to be unemployed than others.

- **The low paid.** The Low Pay Unit argues that low pay is the most important cause of poverty in the UK and estimates that 45% of British workers in 1999 were earning less than two-thirds of the average hourly wage. Low-paid workers are often caught in a **poverty trap** whereby they earn above the minimum level required to claim benefits, but after the deduction of tax, etc., are below it.

  Low pay results from the weakening of workers' legal rights and high levels of unemployment. Changes in the economy have led to increases in the number of mainly female part-time workers and temporary workers. However, New Labour introduced a minimum wage policy in 1999.

- **Women.** Glendinning and Millar (1992) have suggested that society has experienced **a feminisation of poverty** in the last twenty years. This has a number of characteristics:

  - In 1995, 59% of the adult population on income support were female.

  - Income support is the main source of income for single mothers and women pensioners.

  - The number of women in part-time, low-paid and insecure employment has increased substantially in the last decade.

  - They earn only 80% of men's hourly earnings (1996).

  - Women's progress in the labour market is likely to be interrupted by childbirth, child-care and caring for the sick and the old.

  - Women are less likely than men to have made national insurance contributions. They are less likely therefore to be eligible for benefits.

  - Care in the community normally means care by women – which acts as a further obstacle to them entering the labour market.

- **Ethnic minorities.** Black and Asian workers are twice as likely to be unemployed than whites. This may be due to racism and low skill levels.

Theoretical explanations for the causes of poverty

AQA   U2

Individualistic theories

A foundation stone of the Welfare State is the view that some individuals will never be able to care sufficiently for themselves because of age, e.g. children and the elderly, or because of sickness and disability. This approach has probably been the most significant influence on social policy in regard to poverty.

'blaming the victims'

However, modern individualistic theories tend to be critical of people in poverty. They suggest that individuals bring poverty on themselves because they lack initiative and are lazy. David Marsland, a New Right critic of the Welfare State, suggests that welfare benefits have taken away people's sense of personal responsibility. Consequently, people have chosen to be workshy and dependent on welfare benefits.

Cultural theories

'blaming the culture of the victim'

Oscar Lewis argued that some people respond to their position at the bottom of the stratification system by forming fatalistic sub-cultures, within which poverty becomes a way of life. Such values are passed down from generation to generation through socialisation. Children then internalise this culture of poverty and consequently do not take full advantage of changing conditions or improved opportunities which might occur in their lifetime. This theory was very influential in the 1960s and underpinned Operation Headstart, an anti-poverty programme in the USA.

However, the culture of poverty thesis has been criticised on several counts.

- It over-generalises about the behaviour of the poor. Many people are poor but do not behave in the way Lewis describes.

- Madge and Rutter looked for evidence of such a sub-culture in the UK. They concluded 'at least half the children born into a disadvantaged home do not repeat the pattern of disadvantage in the next generation. Over half of all forms of disadvantage arise anew each generation.'

- The fatalistic culture of the poor may be a response to economically adverse conditions, not its cause. Lister and Beresford (1991) argue that the poor subscribe to realist ideas about their situation. These may involve low self-esteem, lack of confidence, depression and feelings of powerlessness due to society stigmatising the poor as scroungers, etc.

'blaming the culture of the victim'

> The New Right underclass theory of Charles Murray developed Lewis' ideas in the 1980s. Murray argues that in the inner city and on council estates a sub-culture exists that he calls an underclass – in which parents encourage their children to be dependent on welfare benefits and crime. Murray suggests the Welfare State is partly to blame for this because it has created a culture of dependency and increased the numbers in the population who expect to be supported by the state and the taxpayer.
>
> KEY POINT

Murray has been accused of blaming the victims of poverty and his critics argue that groups such as the old, the chronically sick and the disabled cannot be blamed for dependence on benefits. Finally, Murray, like Lewis, may be guilty of scapegoating the poor for social problems which are caused by structural factors such as unemployment, racism, the decline of the inner city, etc. Some argue that the behaviour of the poor is constrained by their economic situation.

Marxism

'blaming society'

- Marxists believe that poverty is a **structural characteristic of capitalism.** Ownership of wealth is in the hands of a bourgeoise minority. The rest of society has to share limited economic resources. The problem of poverty is really the problem of inequalities in the distribution of wealth.

  Marxists argue that continuing poverty is in the interests of the ruling class. **Kincaid** notes that employers have a vested interest in cheap labour. Unemployment weakens trade union power and keeps wages low. It also **divides and rules** the working class as they compete for jobs.

  Critics of Marxism argue that it fails to explain why some groups of workers such as women and ethnic minorities are more likely to be in poverty than others. **Townsend** argues that the explanation lies in the **labour market** – most of the poor are unskilled and consequently are unable to compete equally with skilled workers, who are mainly men. Black and female unskilled workers also experience discrimination and are concentrated in a **secondary, low-paid and insecure labour market.**

Progress check

1 What female groups are likely to be in poverty?
2 What does David Marsland blame for poverty?
3 What structural factors do individualistic and cultural theories of poverty ignore?
4 What does Marxism blame for poverty?
5 What causes poverty for black workers and women in the secondary labour market?

5 Discrimination.
4 Capitalism and inequality in the distribution of wealth.
3 Unemployment, poverty, racism, social class, inner-city problems, etc.
2 Welfare benefits.
1 Female pensioners, single mothers, part-time workers, the disabled and full-time carers.

8.2 Welfare

After studying this section you should be able to:

- *identify different social policy solutions to poverty*
- *outline and assess sociological theories about the nature and role of public, private, voluntary and informal welfare provision*

LEARNING SUMMARY

The Welfare State and poverty

 AQA ▶ U2

The term 'Welfare State', refers to the State taking responsibility for welfare provision. G. Marshall (1999) notes that the State offers services and benefits to meet people's basic needs for housing, health, education and income. The Welfare State has its origins in the Poor Law which provided relief for the poor, sick and elderly in the 17th century. During the 19th century, the State gradually grew more involved with the welfare of society through public health provision, e.g. sewers and clean water supplies, and the 1870 Education Act. The Liberal Government of 1906–1914 introduced free school meals, old age pensions for those aged 70 and over, national insurance and limited unemployment benefits. However, the organisation of the present Welfare State and the principles underpinning it have their origin in the Labour Government between 1945–51.

In 1942 the **Beveridge Report** was published with the aim of creating a modern Welfare State and defeating 'five giant evils':

- **want or poverty** – through a universal social security system embracing pensions, unemployment benefit, child benefit and sickness and disability benefits and financed by national insurance. This would be supplemented with a selective means-tested benefit acting as a safety net for those who could not look after themselves, i.e. income support
- **idleness** – the State intended to maintain full employment through intervention in the economy
- **ignorance** or lack of education was to be addressed mainly through the 1944 Education Act, which introduced free secondary education for all
- **squalor** or poor housing was to be addressed through a programme of council house building
- **disease** or poor health would be addressed through the setting up of the National Health Service funded by the State.

The Welfare State, however, is not the sole provider of such services. It has always operated in the context of **welfare pluralism**. Private services exist in the fields of education, health and pensions. The **voluntary sector** also plays a major role in health and welfare, e.g. agencies such as Age Concern. Finally, the **informal sector**, i.e. family care, plays a central role especially in the care of the sick, disabled and elderly.

> *Consensus = agreement between political parties.*

Between 1950 and 1979 there was a good deal of consensus in regard to how Labour and Conservative governments saw the Welfare State. Until the late 1960s both parties intervened in the economy to maintain full employment. There was some movement towards selective benefits in the 1970s as concerns grew about the costs of the Welfare State especially as unemployment rose. Both parties were committed to the **social democratic** view that Welfare State policies were the best way of meeting social needs.

Welfare changes by the Conservative Government 1979–97

The Thatcher government was influenced by thinkers known collectively as the 'New Right', who generally stressed free market principles, self-reliance and individual responsibility. They argued that the rising costs of the Welfare State were interfering with economic growth and that the Welfare State had discouraged personal initiative by creating the conditions for welfare dependency.

> *Contrast these changes with those proposed by New Labour.*

Mrs Thatcher radically overhauled sections of the Welfare State in a number of ways.

- **Selectivity and means testing** were increased – to ensure that those receiving benefits really needed them, e.g. discretionary grants for household items were replaced with loans from a social fund that had to be repaid.
- **Cuts were made in some benefits**, e.g. housing benefit was significantly reduced after 1986. Income support for 16- and 17-year-olds was abolished. The value of benefits did not generally keep up with inflation or average wage levels.

- **Privatisation of services** was actively encouraged. Private companies were encouraged to run old people's homes and local government services such as refuse collection. Council housing was sold off. Private schools and hospitals were encouraged to compete with the public sector. Incentives to opt into private welfare and health schemes were introduced.

- **Charges** were introduced (especially within the NHS) for services traditionally subsidised by the State.

- The introduction of **community care** led to the closing of institutions such as psychiatric and geriatric hospitals and day-care facilities for the severely disabled. Local authorities, families and voluntary organisations are now expected to take a greater responsibility in caring for these groups.

Generally, welfare pluralism became more important as the State retreated from the provision of welfare services.

Theories of the Welfare State

AQA ▸ U2

The Right, or market liberal, critique

Marsland (1989) believes that universal benefits are too costly and result in less capital to invest in the economy. This has partly been responsible for Britain's economic decline during the 1970s and 1980s. Marsland argues that a culture of dependency has eroded the capacity of the unemployed and single mothers to be self-reliant. He believes that **selective benefits** should replace universal benefits and the private sector should be encouraged to provide welfare services.

Jordan (1989) is Marsland's main critic. He points out that universal benefits help maintain a reasonable standard for disadvantaged groups who under a more selective system may be forced to turn to crime or be trapped in a cycle of disadvantage.

The Left critique

Le Grand (1982) notes the Welfare State has failed to redistribute resources from rich to poor and to tackle basic problems such as homelessness and poverty. He argues that the middle classes have benefited from a 'hidden' welfare state in terms of success in the State educational system, state subsidies on mortgages and housing, and improved health and longer life expectancy.

Marxists argue that the Welfare State has benefited the capitalist class in three main ways.

- The Welfare State is an **ideological state apparatus** aiming to convince the working class that they have an 'equal' stake in society – Le Grand points out there is no evidence for such equality. Ginsberg (1979) calls this the 'welfare bribe'. It ensures that the working class do not challenge the fundamental inequalities in wealth and power that characterise capitalism.

- The Welfare State ensures a healthy and literate full-time and part-time 'reserve' workforce.

- Welfare rules have been designed to reinforce labour discipline, e.g. the unemployed have to prove that they are actively seeking work. They face the risk of losing benefits if they turn down training opportunities.

Feminism

Feminist perspectives also focus on the family (Chapter 2) and the feminisation of poverty.

> Feminists argue that the Welfare State functions to **maintain and reproduce patriarchy**. The benefit system has tended to assume that women are economically dependent upon men and that women's main role is in the home as a mother and housewife. This has been crucial in the support of the nuclear family ideal. **Benston** argues that such a family is **central to the maintenance of capitalism** because it produces the future workforce free of charge and maintains the health and efficiency of the present one. Moreover, women's labour (especially in relation to caring for the sick, disabled and the elderly) means that the Welfare State actually costs a great deal less than it should.

New Labour and welfare

AQA ▶ U2

Contrast with Conservative policy.

When New Labour came to office in 1997 it announced that in terms of spending and taxation, little would change. However, a number of policy changes relating to the Welfare State were announced:

- The **Social Exclusion Unit** was set up, based on the idea that a number of social groups such as single mothers, the unemployed, the homeless and those living on deprived housing estates are socially excluded from participating in society. Its remit is to come up with solutions to integrate these groups into society.

- The 'New Deal' is one such policy. This aims to reduce poverty and the cost of welfare by assisting the unemployed and single mothers to find employment. These 'welfare to work' policies have included job advice interviews, help with child-care costs, encouragement to re-enter education or to embark upon re-training programmes, and the introduction of a **national minimum wage**.

- A **Working Families Tax Credit** was introduced in 1998. This encourages return to work and employment because it supplements earned incomes.

- **Private stake-holder pensions** have been encouraged to top up the state pension. Pension credits will be given to family carers who have been unable to accrue pension rights through work.

Progress check

1 Identify Beveridge's five giant evils.
2 What is the difference between universal and selective systems of benefits?
3 What is welfare pluralism?
4 What group makes up the informal sector of welfare provision?
5 What is the hidden welfare state?
6 What is the welfare bribe?

6 The ideology that the Welfare State primarily benefits working-class people. In reality it does not.
5 The benefits the middle classes have taken from free education and the NHS.
4 The family.
3 A situation in which the State sector, the voluntary sector, the informal sector and private sector combine to provide welfare services.
2 Universal are paid to all, e.g. child benefit is paid to all with children. Selective benefits are means-tested and paid to the most needy.
1 Want, Squalor, Ignorance, Idleness and Disease.

Sample question and model answer

A typical AQA question.

You will have 1 hour and 15 minutes. Spend 15 minutes reading the data and planning your responses.

1 hour should be spent writing.

Questions will always be based on this format.

Don't over-respond to questions and in terms of time spent and length.

Item A

The levels of poverty are not randomly distributed across the population but disproportionately affect particular social groups. Owing to discrimination in employment, women are more likely to be found in part-time work on low wages and with little job security. The Welfare State requires women to take responsibility for unpaid work in the home. Paid employment is permitted but jobs taken up by women tend to mirror roles in the home. These too are low paid. In consequence women as a group are much more likely to be excluded from acceptable standards of living. Lone mothers are at particular risk of falling onto the breadline.

Adapted from T. Spybey (ed.), Britain in Europe, *Routledge, 1997*

Item B

Charles Booth defined absolute poverty as having barely sufficient means for a decent independent life. He saw poverty as a struggle to obtain the necessaries of life and make ends meet. He saw the very poor as living in a state of chronic want.

Kenneth Galbraith defined relative poverty as not having what the larger community regards as the minimum necessary for decency. The poor live outside grades or categories which the community regard as acceptable.

a) Explain what is meant by subsistence poverty. [2 marks]

a) Subsistence poverty is absolute poverty – the idea that a minimum standard for survival can be worked out using criteria such as diet.

b) Identify and briefly explain two of Beveridge's five giant evils. [4 marks]

b) Squalor referred to homelessness or slum housing conditions. In regard to the latter, a slum clearance programme in the 1950s and 1960s was paralleled by the building of council houses.

Ignorance referred to the lack of education, experienced by working-class children after the age of 14. The 1944 Education Act introduced free secondary education for all.

c) Suggest three reasons why women are more likely than men to be found in poverty. [6 marks]

c) They are more likely to be elderly widowed pensioners.
Ninety per cent of lone parents are women.
They are more likely than men to be in low paid, part-time and insecure work.

d) Identify and discuss two characteristics of consensus definitions of poverty. [8 marks]

d) It is based on asking the general population what they think are necessaries for a decent standard of living rather than relying on the subjective interpretations of a sociologist.

It was able to adjust for changes in standard of living between 1983 and 1990 as the consensus changed in regard to standards and social expectations.

Sample question and model answer (continued)

Note instruction to use Item A.

You should spend 20 minutes on this section.

Note references to Item A.

e) Using information from Item A and elsewhere, examine the view that social policy has tended to neglect the feminisation of poverty. [20 marks]

e) There is considerable evidence that social policy has tended to neglect the feminisation of poverty: 62% of adults who receive income support are women. As Item A notes, the jobs taken up by women tend to mirror roles in the home. They generally tend to be low paid. According to the Labour Force Survey (1995) 5.2 million women are in part-time employment. These make up a substantial majority of low-paid workers. Item A also points out that the Welfare State expects women to take unpaid labour in the home. Consequently some women will be economically dependent upon their male partner. Peter Townsend argues that these trends indicate a feminisation of poverty.

In addition to low-paid workers, Townsend notes three other female-dominated groups in poverty. First, single mothers – 90% of single-parent families are female-headed. In 1992 approximately 75% of single mothers were claiming income support. This group is less likely to be employed than married mothers. The lack of free child-care is a particular problem because it results in single mothers being excluded from the job opportunities open to other groups.

A second female group in poverty are women pensioners, especially those who live alone. Three times as many women as men over pension age receive income support. Women are likely to be poor pensioners because of previous low earnings, interrupted working careers and greater life expectancy. Pensioners are more likely than most other groups to experience poverty because of rising living standards.

Townsend's third group are women carers who are unable to take jobs because they are responsible for children, the elderly and the sick and disabled. It can be argued that social policy in the form of community care has increased the burden for female carers. Finch and Groves conclude that in practice community care is unpaid female labour which is poorly supported by the State. Women carers also find their employment opportunities are sacrificed in the process. It can be difficult to re-enter the labour market and they will have lost years of pension rights. Community care therefore has tended to confirm gender inequality.

Contemporary material.

Social policy, pre-1997, did not tackle the feminisation of poverty with any seriousness. However, New Labour has recognised that women are likely to be socially excluded from participating fully in society. Therefore a number of policy measures are aimed specifically at females. The 'New Deal' aims to reduce poverty and the cost of welfare by assisting the unemployed and single mothers to find employment. These 'welfare to work' policies have included job advice interviews, help with child-care costs, encouragement to re-enter education or to embark upon re-training programmes and the introduction of a national minimum wage.

Use Item B. 20 minutes required.

f) Using information from Item B and other sources, evaluate the different methods used by sociologists to measure the degree of poverty in the UK. [20 marks]

f) In Item B Charles Booth defined poverty as a struggle to obtain the necessaries of life and make ends meet. He saw the very poor as living in a state of chronic want. This view was shared by Seebohm Rowntree's (1899) study of poverty in York in the late nineteenth century which used

Sample question and model answer *(continued)*

a subsistence or absolute definition of poverty to measure chronic want. Rowntree worked out a minimum standard of living required for basic survival in terms of diet, clothing and housing. In 1899, Rowntree found that 15% of York's population were living in primary poverty. This meant that they had insufficient earnings to meet even their most basic needs. When he repeated this study in 1936 and 1950 he found that this figure had fallen to approximately 7% and 3%, respectively.

The absolute definition of poverty is thought to have a number of strengths. As a definition, it is clear and unambiguous. It is not confused by degrees of poverty. It states very simply that if people lack specific resources, they are poor. It also has a moral and emotive impact. Absolute stresses the minimum required for survival. Most people would therefore agree that something needs to be done about it.

Use Item B.

In Item B, Kenneth Galbraith defined poverty as not having what the larger community regards as the minimum necessary for decency. Peter Townsend (1979) agrees with this relative definition. Townsend sees resources such as income, housing, education, health and other social services as basic psychological rights necessary for a decent life. As a relativist, Townsend argued that definitions of poverty should not be fixed – they should reflect what the larger community regard as acceptable living standards.

Use of different models indicates evaluation by contrast.

His (1979) national survey of 2000 households asked questions about 60 indicators of deprivation relating to diet, housing, amenities, etc. Townsend concluded that over 40 of his 60 indicators indicated a strong relationship between deprivation and income. Using this relative measurement he concluded that 22.9% of the population were living in poverty. A variation on Townsend's approach was the social consensus approach of the 'Breadline Britain' surveys carried out by Joanna Mack and Stewart Lansley in 1983 and 1990. Mack and Lansley asked a representative sample of ordinary people what they felt were 'necessities'. When the study was repeated in 1990, they found that the number in poverty had increased to one in five of the population. The relativist measurement has the strength of revealing changes in both the standard of living of a society and its cultural expectations. Consequently, sociologists are able to chart the evolution of deprivation.

However, there could be some explicit criticism of the relative model.

Practice examination questions

Item A

There are four key features of the underclass: it suffers multiple deprivation, it is socially marginal, it is almost entirely dependent upon state welfare provisions and its culture is one of resigned fatalism.

This is a client class wholly dependent on state welfare. In such a crippling role of absolute dependency, it is impossible to sustain a positive self image. This class has been disabled by a welfare state which claims to be helping them. The culture of fatalism which develops out of this is generally referred to as a culture of poverty. Negative attitudes and values are reproduced from one generation to the next. Inactivity breeds apathy, the unemployed become unemployable and even when jobs are found they are swiftly lost.

Source: Adapted from P. Saunders, Social Class and Stratification, *Routledge, 1990*

Item B

Dual labour-market theory suggests that there is a primary market characterised by relatively high wages, job security and promotion opportunities and a secondary labour market which is characterised by low wages, little job security and few possibilities for promotion.

Barron and Norris point out that groups in poverty such as women are more likely to get jobs in the secondary sector because employers ascribe characteristics to females which make them seem suited to these types of jobs. They are seen as easy to replace, less concerned about wage levels and less interested in promotion because of their commitment to family life.

1 Explain what is meant by welfare dependency. [2 marks]

2 In your own words, identify two characteristics of the underclass. [4 marks]

3 Suggest three reasons why ethnic minorities are likely to be part of the secondary labour market. [6 marks]

4 Identify and explain two criticisms of the culture of poverty thesis. [8 marks]

5 Using Item A and other sources, critically examine New Right views on the relationship between inequality and welfare. [20 marks]

6 Using information from Item B and elsewhere, evaluate the view that poverty is an inevitable feature of the way society is organised. [20 marks]

Chapter 9

Work and leisure

The following topics are covered in this chapter:

- *The organisation of work*
- *Non-work*

9.1 The organisation of work

Work, industrialism and capitalism

AQA U2

In order to understand work and leisure, we must consider the two powerful forces shaping the conditions in which work and leisure take place: industrialism and capitalism.

'Industrialism' can be defined as the mechanised production of goods by workers in large workplaces. Workers perform specialised tasks although the speed and nature of their work is determined by technology. Control of workers and the work process is co-ordinated by specialised managers.

'Capitalism' can be defined 'as the financing of economic activity by the investment of capital in the expectation of making a profit, and is characterised by the private ownership of the means of production and wage labour'. (Fulcher and Scott, 1999).

> The economies of Western societies are **industrial capitalist**. Fulcher and Scott note that capitalism's pursuit of greater profit resulted in the transformation of work and industry as mass-production techniques were developed. The most successful of these techniques was **Fordism** – a system of mass production organised around assembly-line production by the car manufacturer, Henry Ford, between 1908–14. The development of industrial capitalism led to the parallel development of 'leisure' as daily life was divided into work and non-work.
>
> **KEY POINT**

In capitalist societies, work tends to be defined as 'waged labour'. It takes place within a formal economy recognised by the State and subject to control through mechanisms such as tax. Paid work confers identity and status on workers. It also provides access to a network of social relationships. The supremacy of wage labour often means that there are negative consequences for the unemployed and retired. Non-work often means loss of status and identity which may not be compensated for by leisure time.

Domestic work provides services within the family and household. It is mainly performed by women, e.g. housework/child-care. Feminists note that it is rarely defined as 'real work' because it is unpaid, and that the distinction between work and leisure is clearer for men than it is for women.

Work and technology in capitalist societies

 AQA ▶ U2

Max Weber saw industrial society as generally positive because it was characterised by the rationalisation of work and social life (Weber saw behaviour influenced by tradition or personal emotion as irrational and inefficient). Productive work is efficient because it is organised according to rational rules, with hierarchies of responsibility and authority.

> **KEY POINT**
>
> Karl **Marx** was critical of the way industrial capitalism had transformed the nature of work. He argued that in pre-industrial society, workers controlled the means of production and work was a creative, fulfilling activity. In capitalist societies, the production and manufacture of goods is financed by owners of private capital. They own the means of production and control the organisation of the work process. Those without wealth are forced to sell their labour power to the capitalist class. Therefore, according to Marx, work has become **a commodity to be bought and sold** rather than an activity fulfilling human needs. The way work is organised is based on the need to extract maximum effort and profitability from labour at minimum cost. Marx saw technology as a means of controlling workers and raising profits because it saved labour costs, reduced skills and thereby increased control by owners and management.

De-skilling

The Marxist, **Harry Braverman (1974)** argues that work is being subjected to progressive **degradation** and **de-skilling**. This process began with Ford's assembly-line, mass-production techniques which broke down complex skills into simplistic routine tasks. However, Braverman argues that de-skilling was accelerated by **F.W. Taylor's Principles of Scientific Management (1947)** which argued that all decision-making should be taken away from workers. Such work-study techniques have been used to re-design the labour process and separate execution from conception (methods, procedures, routine and tools have been taken over by management). Such de-skilling reduces the bargaining power of workers because unskilled workers are easier to replace. De-skilling, therefore, is a **capitalist control strategy** over the labour process.

Braverman argues that in the 1960s and 1970s de-skilling was accelerated by **new technology**, especially computers. Moreover, the process is being extended to white-collar work and commercial organisations such as banks. **Crompton and Jones (1984)** examined the effects of computer technology on white-collar workers and found that clerical work had been fragmented into low-skilled and routine tasks which served to centralise control within the organisation.

Braverman has been criticised for over-stating the influence of Taylorism and de-skilling. Strong trade-union representation and good wages may compensate workers for lack of control over the labour process. There may be management strategies for controlling workers other than technical control.

Other management strategies include 'responsible autonomy' – workers work in teams and control the pace of work.

Post-industrialism

Post-industrialism = decline of manufacturing sector, rise of service sector.

> Daniel **Bell** argues that modern industrial economies have now moved into a **post-industrial** phase, characterised by a transformation in work. The service sector engaged in the processing of knowledge and information is increasing dramatically. Consequently, professionals are becoming the largest sector of the workforce – e.g. there are now more university lecturers than coal-miners in the UK. Knowledge is now the major resource of a post-industrial information society.

KEY POINT

Bell's critics accuse him of exaggerating the extent of change and argue that the service sector may just represent a new stage in industrial development rather than a radically new society. For example, the Marxist, **Ernest Mandel** argues that capitalism has found the service sector a more profitable area for investment than manufacturing. Many large transnationals have diversified into services when manufacturing profits have been threatened. Moreover, the processing of information has always been a foundation of industrial production.

Post-Fordist, or flexible specialisation, theory

This theory argues that there is a radical shift occurring in the way work is organised in industrial societies. Inflexible technology and the rigid division of labour associated with Fordism are giving way to more 'flexible' methods of production because modern societies require greater diversity and range in products. Demand for exclusive products for particular groups or lifestyles is allegedly increasing.

Flexible production has a number of characteristics according to Atkinson (1985) and Warde (1989).

- **Computer-based technologies** have evolved which can be adapted to the requirements of rapidly changing products and designs.
- Workers are acquiring **functional flexibility**. They are now more likely to be multi-skilled, highly motivated and adaptable. This challenges Braverman's de-skilling thesis.
- Management has undergone **de-centralisation** in order to create a team spirit conducive to the flexible production of quality products.
- Companies have adopted the policy of '**numerical flexibility**'. The core workforce is supplemented by a **peripheral workforce** made up of temporary full-time workers and part-timers. The use of short-term contracts is becoming a norm.

However, in criticism **Thompson (1993)** argues that manual workers have undergone training in '**multi-tasking**' so that they can work effectively on simple tasks on any section of an assembly line. This supports Braverman's ideas.

Other critics of Post-Fordism argue that the decline of mass production has been exaggerated. In particular, the **globalisation** of mass production has been neglected. Companies have relocated to less developed countries because of the low costs of production.

Feminist views of work

Sylvia Walby suggests Post-Fordists don't address the issue of gender and work. She argues that the growth of the part-time workforce represents an employer strategy to exploit women more effectively and to undermine trade-union power. Others have suggested that a flexible workforce means a **casual workforce**. This may be an employer strategy to control the workforce and keep wage costs down rather than a response to the need for new production techniques. Finally, Pollert (1988) argues that capitalism has always used a peripheral workforce. It merely represents capitalism's constant search to cut costs and increase profits.

Neo-Fordism

Marxist influenced.

This theory argues that we are experiencing a new phase of capitalism rather than a transformation of it. These theorists agree that modern industrial economies are moving away from mass production to small-scale and flexible production. However, they argue that this is a gradual process. They see de-skilling and managerial control as increasing. More is now demanded of workers in terms of quality, range of tasks and time at work. Neo-Fordists are less optimistic about the peripheral workforce's conditions of service and see this trend as 'coercive pacification' – suppressing industrial conflict by weakening trade unions and collective bargaining.

Progress check

1 What system characterises the economies of Western societies?
2 What is the function of technology according to Marx?
3 What is de-skilling?
4 What is Taylorism?
5 What does Daniel Bell argue?
6 What is the difference between Post-Fordism and Neo-Fordism?
7 What is multi-tasking?

7 The ability to work on any task at any point of the assembly line or work process.
6 Post-Fordists argue that industrial production has evolved from mass production techniques to more flexible methods. Neo-Fordists suggest this is just another capitalist technique for increasing profits.
5 That industrial society has moved into a post-industrial phase in which the production of knowledge is more important than manufacturing.
4 The removal of decision-making from workers. All work processes are controlled by management.
3 The breaking down of complex skilled tasks into routine simple tasks which require little training, usually with the aid of technology.
2 To control workers and enhance profits.
1 Industrial capitalism.

Attitudes to work

AQA   U2

The Marxist view

Marx argued that in pre-industrial society, work was creative and a means by which human beings expressed themselves. However, in capitalist societies only a few individuals are allowed the freedom to express themselves in their work. This is because the capitalist class controls the labour process. As a result, work is alien to the worker – a means to an end rather than an end in itself. Work becomes merely a means of staying alive.

Marx argued that alienation is the main evil of capitalism. Workers are alienated wage slaves cut off from their work. The competitive nature of capitalism and the organisation of production also cuts them off from other workers. They are unable to identify with the products of their labour because they only play a partial role in their production. Marx argued that even workers who are satisfied with their jobs are alienated. This is because alienation is an objective state (rather than a subjective state) created by the relationship of the worker to the means of production. The only solution is a communist mode of production, which allows workers to work for themselves and others at the same time. People share the rewards of their labour and fulfil their needs as workers and human beings.

Robert Blauner

Blauner argued that this Marxist concept of alienation was too vague to measure empirically. He also rejected the Marxist view that alienation was exclusively an objective state. He stressed that subjective feelings about levels of satisfaction were a key criteria in the measurement of alienation. Blauner also saw alienation as objectively related to the type of technology used at work.

According to Blauner, alienation has four dimensions which he attempted to measure using questionnaires assessing worker attitudes and behaviour. These are:

* powerlessness – workers may feel that they have no influence on management and no control over their conditions of employment and the actual work process
* meaninglessness – workers may feel that there is very little sense of purpose in their job
* isolation – workers may not feel part of a wider work community
* self-estrangement – workers may feel unable to express themselves through their work or feel involved in it.

Blauner examined four types of work technology:

* craft, e.g. printing
* machine technology, e.g. textiles
* assembly-line, mass-production, e.g. car plants
* continuous production technology, in which machines process the product whilst workers monitor and control the machines.

Blauner found the lowest level of alienation in craft technology, alienation increased with machine and assembly-line technology and decreased with continuous production technology. Blauner saw continuous production technology as the future of capitalism because it made work satisfying and meaningful again as workers felt they had control over their working environment. He predicted its high levels of satisfaction would reduce the industrial conflict which he saw as being rooted in alienation.

Blauner's methodology has been criticised. It is notoriously difficult to operationalise the concepts of 'satisfaction' and 'alienation' in questionnaires. Moreover, his examples of industries have become very dated. Printing can no longer be considered a craft technology in this day and age. Grint notes that very few workers in the car industry actually work on assembly lines. Beynon and Nichols', (1977) study of continuous production technology in a chemical plant in SE England found high levels of boredom among technicians.

Supports Marx.

Huw Beynon's (1973) study of a Ford Motor plant used participant observation on the shop-floor and interviews with managers and workers. He found that managers used production technology to get more work out of workers, thus reducing labour costs, improving productivity and increasing profits, e.g. managers often increased the speed of the assembly line. Beynon agreed with the Marxist position that technology was a tool of exploitation used by management to control workers. Its role as a source of alienation was secondary to this. Marxists argue that the primary source of alienation is the organisation of capitalism. Consequently, in the workplace there is a struggle between managers and workers. The result is conflict and the potential for strikes and industrial sabotage.

Goldthorpe and Lockwood's (1969) work orientations

Critical of Marx.

These two are critical of the Marxist concept of alienation, arguing that conflicts at work are based on limited economic goals (i.e. demand for higher pay). Few workers are interested in questioning the legitimacy of capitalism. According to Goldthorpe and Lockwood, the experience of work will depend on how workers define work. This depends upon their 'work-orientation', i.e. their motives for working.

A Weberian prospective.

> In their study of **affluent workers** (1968), Goldthorpe and Lockwood found that assembly-line workers were least satisfied with work but technology was not the cause. Work orientation was the deciding factor. Affluent workers were home- and family-centred. They subscribed to an **instrumental** orientation to work – it was seen as a means of improving living standards. They therefore did not look for satisfaction at work nor did they expect it. Instead, satisfaction was looked for and found in the home and family. However, Goldthorpe and Lockwood's sample of mainly married men with dependent children may not be representative of most manual workers. Their sample also received wages well above the national average. They also fail to explain the origin of these instrumental attitudes.

KEY POINT

Duncan Gallie (1978)

Gallie also focused on factors outside the workplace, studying two chemical plants, one in England and the other in France. He noted that chemical workers in these two different countries had very different histories, cultures and union organisation. In France, management was more autocratic whilst in Britain workers were more likely to be consulted and involved in decisions. Consequently, French chemical plants were characterised by more conflict between management and workers.

Feminist views on alienation

Feminists argue that studies of alienation neglect women even though women tend to be over-represented in assembly-line production. Married women have the dual burden of alienating housework and manual work. Crompton and Jones' (1984) study of female white-collar workers found that automation had increased alienation for these workers although frequent contact with the general public partly compensated for this. They did find some evidence that women had different orientations to work compared with men, e.g. as women got older and took on the family roles of marriage and children, they were less likely to feel dissatisfied with, for example, lack of promotion possibilities than men .

Conflict at work

Industrial conflict

Industrial conflict refers specifically to the conflict of interest between the owners of capital and wage labour. Dahrendorf argues that class conflict in the workplace has become institutionalised through collective bargaining. Trade unions act as interest groups both in the workplace and wider society representing the interests of workers to employers and governments. Consequently, the working class are now integrated into the capitalist system and can influence decision-making. However, Marxists are critical of this idea. They claim collective bargaining is a form of **capitalist social control**. It legitimates class conflict in the workplace and wider society by reducing it to a narrow set of aims focusing on wages, hours of work and working conditions. This does not threaten the capitalist economic and social order and has largely failed to improve the economic position of trade-union members.

There are different types of industrial conflict.

- **Strikes** are the most obvious and publicised but are relatively rare. Daniel and Millward's (1983) study of 2000 establishments found that only 25% had experienced any industrial action.
- Workers may refuse to work overtime. They may insist on working to rule.
- Discontent can also take the form of absenteeism, resignation, industrial sabotage and theft.

KEY POINT

Statistics on strikes are problematical. Official definitions only include strikes which last a full day or involve at least 10 workers or lead to a loss of 100 working days or more. Therefore not all strikes are reported to the Department of Employment.

Reasons for industrial conflict are as follows.

- The **isolated mass theory** of Kerr and Siegel (1954) argued that the relative isolation of occupational communities from wider society, e.g. miners, dockers and seamen, may be an influence. These groups have a strong sense of working-class solidarity favourable to trade unions and collective action, e.g. strikes in Britain have tended to concentrate on mining, iron and steel and the car industry. Occupational communities probably help develop the community resolve required to win industrial action.
- **Edwards and Scullion (1982)** found a range of reasons for industrial conflict across different industries. **Boredom and overbearing managers** were blamed in the textile industry for high labour turnover and absenteeism. Less industrial conflict was found in industries in which workers were consulted.
- Evidence indicates that workers see **wage disputes** as the main reason for conflict. These may provide legitimation for other grievances such as poor management.

KEY POINT

- Beynon argues that workers often see strikes as about resisting social control by managers.
- Marxists see strikes as disputes over scarce resources in capitalist societies characterised by class inequalities in wealth, income and power. However, this does not explain variations in industrial conflict between different groups of workers.

The 1980s and 1990s have seen a decline in the power of trade unions and collective bargaining. Moreover, 1979–1996 saw a dramatic fall in union membership.

The decline of trade unions

New Labour's attitude towards the trade unions?

When Mrs Thatcher was elected, she set about reducing the power of the unions by introducing legislation which restricted the ability of trade unions to take effective industrial action. The law was changed so that trade unions had to have secret ballots on industrial action and the election of senior officers. Secondary industrial action was outlawed. Funds could be confiscated for breaking these laws.

Recession in the primary and secondary sectors of the economy, and high levels of unemployment, also reduced the bargaining power of trade unions. Employers took advantage of these conditions. There was a movement towards individual bargaining and the bypassing of trade unions. In some industries, employers refused to recognise trade unions. Flexible rates of pay rather than fixed rates, no strike deals and more flexible working practices were agreed to by some trade unions.

Progress check

1 How does Marx define alienation?

2 Identify the four dimensions of alienation according to Blauner.

3 What technology is the future of capitalism according to Blauner?

4 What is the purpose of technology according to Beynon?

5 What is the biggest influence on satisfaction at work according to Goldthorpe and Lockwood?

6 Identify three types of industrial action in addition to strikes.

7 How do Goldthorpe and Lockwood and Huw Beynon explain strikes?

7 The former suggest wage disputes are the main cause, whilst Beynon suggests strikes are a means of resistance to management control.
6 Any from: work to rule, refusal to work overtime, absenteeism, industrial sabotage, resignation and theft.
5 Orientation to work.
4 To control the workforce.
3 Continuous production techniques.
2 Powerlessness, meaninglessness, isolation and self estrangement.
1 As being cut off from work, the product of labour and from other workers.

9.2 Non-work

After studying this section you should be able to:

- *explain the causes of unemployment and describe its social consequences*
- *describe leisure patterns*
- *outline and assess different sociological theories of leisure*
- *discuss the relationship between leisure, identity and consumption*

LEARNING SUMMARY

Unemployment

 AQA   U2

The official way of measuring unemployment has changed thirty-three times since 1979. At the moment, it is based upon the number of people who actually claim unemployment-related benefits. This excludes 16–17 year olds on training schemes. It also excludes anyone not eligible to claim such benefits, such as women whose partners are working and single mothers. To claim benefit, the claimant must prove that they are actively seeking work. Unemployment statistics, then, are regarded as notoriously unreliable.

> However, some social characteristics of the unemployed can be identified:
>
> - They are likely to be **unskilled**.
>
> - They may **belong to an ethnic minority**, e.g. the Pakistani/Bangladeshi unemployment rate is three times that of whites.
>
> - They are likely to be **aged between 16–19**. This age group for males has an unemployment rate nearly three times that of all males.

KEY POINT

Explanations for unemployment

- J.M. Keynes blamed **lack of demand** in the economy, e.g. less money to spend reduces demand for goods. This leads to reduced profits and job losses. State intervention in the form of economic investment could create jobs by increasing people's spending power. Demand for goods should then increase and unemployment should fall.

- Market Liberals and New Right thinkers believe that **too much state intervention** is the cause. They believe that this interferes with the freedom of the market for goods, services and labour. Unemployment is also encouraged by the high rate of benefits which leads to **less incentive to work**.

- Marxism argues that unemployment is an **inevitable feature of capitalism**. There are two aspects to this theory:

  - Marx believed **periodic crises** are a cyclical feature of capitalism.

  - **New technologies** introduced to boost productivity and reduce labour costs result in de-skilling and therefore unemployment. However, critics point out that the introduction of new technology has been an on-going process since the Industrial Revolution. It can be argued that automation also creates work and new occupations.

Very important – car companies, in particular, relocate to the third world.

- **Globalisation** in the form of increasing international competition from the low-cost economies of the Third World and tiger economies of South East Asia is increasingly blamed.

The social consequences of unemployment

It is difficult to untangle the effects of unemployment from the effects of other factors associated with unemployment, e.g. poverty. Different people also experience unemployment in different ways. However, it can have the following effects:

Suicide too.

> **KEY POINT**
>
> - poverty
> - psychological effects such as depression, low self-esteem, loss of identity and feelings of powerlessness
> - family problems, such as high divorce rates
> - ill health
> - social problems such as crime and delinquency and social unrest such as urban riots. These can be an indirect product of unemployment, but it is difficult to prove these links.

Leisure

AQA   U2

Defining leisure

Leisure generally means the time in which individuals are free from other social obligations, especially work. Fulcher and Scott suggest it is normally 'a time of freedom, individual choice, self-expression and creativity'. However, it is not a straightforward phenomenon to define. Parker (1971) points out that work and leisure are only two categories of 'life space'. There are also 'intermediate categories' such as eating, sleeping and attending to hygiene, which are physiological needs.

E.P. Thompson (1967) suggests industrialisation is responsible for the division of time into work and leisure. According to S. Parker, the major influence on leisure is work. He notes three types of relationship between work and leisure:

> **KEY POINT**
>
> - the extension pattern – work spills over into leisure time. People who fit this pattern generally enjoy their work
> - the neutrality pattern – family life and leisure are the major life interests because work is generally unfulfilling and even alienating
> - the opposition, or segmentalist, pattern – leisure compensates for the hazards and physical demands of dangerous jobs.

Parker is criticised for ignoring other factors which impact on leisure, e.g. the influence of the lifestyles of class sub-cultures on leisure patterns. He also neglects the leisure patterns of women, i.e. he fails to examine the impact of housework and motherhood on women's experience of leisure.

Marxist theories of leisure

The Neo-Marxists, Clarke and Critcher (1985), suggest leisure is structured and constrained by capitalism. They argue that the three most important influences on leisure are as follows.

- The State plays a central role in regulating leisure activities through the law and policing of public space such as streets and parks. The State also promotes and subsidises bourgeois leisure activities as more 'civilised' and worthy than working-class activities.

- The leisure industry has been transformed by capitalism into a commodity, and consumers of leisure are exploited in a similar way to workers. For example, working-class pubs have been commercialised by big business in the form of brewers. Such leisure industries create false leisure needs using intensive media and advertising campaigns.

- The material conditions of the working class prevent them making real leisure choices. They may lack the resources to join health clubs, play golf and visit the ballet.

Feminist theories of leisure

McIntosh (1987) notes that most theories of leisure neglect the influence of gender, arguing that men and women take part in very different types of leisure activity. Women tend to have less access to leisure activities than men – probably because men have more time and financial resources for leisure. Most time outside paid work for women with children is not leisure time but dominated by domestic responsibilities. These often blur the distinction between work and leisure for women. Green, Hebron and Woodward (1987) suggest that women's leisure is constrained by patriarchal influences outside the home too, e.g. fear of attack at night narrows leisure options in the public sphere for women.

Post-modern theories of leisure

> **KEY POINT**
>
> These focus on the consumption patterns of individuals. They suggest that the individual has many more leisure choices because of new technologies, especially in the field of media. This is reinforced by the globalisation of culture via the new technologies of digital and satellite television and the Internet. Leisure experience is no longer tied to a particular time or place. People now use leisure time and activities to construct unique lifestyles and social identities for themselves. They are no longer constrained by social class, gender and ethnicity.

Critics such as Scraton and Braham (1995) note that the constraints of class, gender and ethnicity are still very influential. For many women, leisure remains influenced by little disposable income, jobs with anti-social hours and domestic responsibilities, making access to formal leisure difficult, if not impossible. Social class also constrains – access to post-modern forms of leisure is heavily dependent on a relatively high income. Ethnicity, too, is a constraint – high unemployment, poverty in inner-city areas and racism negatively affect leisure choices. Often ethnic lifestyles and identities are not a result of choice but a rational form of resistance and survival strategies in the face of racism.

Progress check

1 How many times has the official method of measuring unemployment changed since 1979?

2 Which groups are not included in official definitions of unemployment?

3 What does Parker mean by the extension pattern of leisure?

4 Who argues that leisure has become a commodity to be exploited for profit?

5 Who does McIntosh claim most theories of leisure neglect?

6 What do post-modern theories of leisure focus on?

6 Consumption patterns and lifestyle choices.

5 Women.

4 The Marxists, Clarke and Critcher.

3 Work becomes part of leisure time.

2 16–17-year-olds on training schemes, housewives, single mothers.

1 33 times.

Sample question and model answer

A typical AQA question.

You will have 1 hour and 15 minutes. Spend 15 minutes reading the data and planning your response.

Item A

According to Harry Braverman, routine white-collar work is being subjected to the same de-skilling processes that have characterised manufacturing. He reports that young well-educated workers in the USA are alienated by low-paid, routinised clerical jobs. Pride in work which was once creative and challenging has now been replaced by the boredom and monotony of de-skilled repetitive labour.

In the UK, the evidence for these processes is mixed. Certainly in the financial sector, GB has experienced 'downsizing' in the wake of mergers and recession. There is evidence that technology is de-skilling the clerical sector. Instead of a career, the new-age bank clerk has a job. Because such a job demands relatively little training and provides little chance of career development, it hardly offers a lifetime's employment. However, Penn (1994) found contradictory evidence showing many workers, especially full-time female workers, derived great satisfaction from their jobs.

1 hour should be spent writing.

Item B

Economic activity, i.e. percentage in work by ethnic group.

Ethnic Group %	Age (in years)					Males aged 16–64	Females aged 16–59
	16–19	20–29	30–39	40–49	50–59/64		
White	62.0	82.1	84.5	86.7	69.0	86.1	71.9
Black	41.7	75.2	75.2	87.3	70.3	80.4	66.0
Indian	25.1	72.5	77.6	86.3	61.3	80.8	61.4
Pakistani/ Bangladeshi	35.4	52.8	52.1	50.2	41.1	72.3	24.8
Other	47.0	60.0	68.7	84.3	75.5	76.0	58.6
All ethnic groups	60.1	81.0	83.5	86.4	68.7	85.6	70.8

Source: Social Trends 24 (Crown Copyright) 1994

Don't over-respond to questions a–d in terms of time spent and length.

a) Explain what is meant by de-skilling. [2 marks]

a) The breaking down of complex skilled tasks into routine simple tasks which require little training.

b) Suggest two factors which may be leading to the de-skilling of white-collar work. [4 marks]

Two from:

b) The drive to greater profit may lead to employers breaking down expensive scarce skills into cheaper and more routinised tasks – this saves costs. The development of automation and technology such as computers means that complex tasks can be performed by machines. The desire to reduce trade union power and the bargaining power of workers. The need to exert greater control over workers.

c) Identify three groups likely to be employed. [6 marks]

c) The unskilled.

The Pakistani/Bangladeshi unemployment rate is three times that of whites. Young people aged between 16–19. This age group for males has an unemployment rate nearly three times that of all males.

Sample question and model answer (continued)

d) Identify and discuss two dimensions of alienation which Blauner might use to measure low job satisfaction in white-collar work.   [8 marks]

d) Powerlessness: White-collar workers could be asked via a questionnaire or interviews how they feel in regard to their influence on management. Whether or not they feel they have control over their conditions of employment and the actual work process could also be explored.

Meaninglessness, i.e. whether workers feel a sense of purpose in their job, especially in the light of de-skilling and new technology could be explored using informal interviews. Questions about commitment, loyalty, security may produce data which uncovers whether workers find their jobs meaningful.

Crompton and Jones' (1984) study of female white-collar workers found that automation had increased alienation for these workers, although frequent contact with the general public partly compensated for this.

> You should spend 20 minutes on this question.

e) Using Item A and other sources, assess the view that clerical work and middle management jobs are increasingly being de-skilled by new technology.

[20 marks]

> Reference to Item A.

e) The idea that clerical and middle-management occupations have been de-skilled originates with the American Marxist, Harry Braverman. In Item A, he argues that while the number of white-collar jobs has increased, the skills required to do the jobs has been reduced. He states that clerks once had wide-ranging responsibilities but as companies grew larger during the twentieth century, so clerical work was reorganised so that workers specialised in fewer tasks. Computerisation speeded up this process. The office consequently argues Braverman became like a production line for mental work as clerical work became highly regulated. The skills required of the clerical workforce, which is now mainly female, are now minimal. Consequently clerical workers have become proletarianised – they share a similar economic and social status with the working class. They now have jobs rather than careers. Braverman also suggests that similar processes are occurring in middle-management positions. He claims that engineers, accountants and teachers are increasingly finding their jobs are more closely regulated and their power, pay and privileges eroded. Unemployment is increasing for such workers who once enjoyed 'safe and secure' careers.

> Assessment.

There is some evidence supporting Braverman. Crompton and Jones' study of bank workers found strong evidence that clerical workers no longer exercised control over how they worked. De-skilling was evident in that clerks simply followed a set of routines. Crompton and Jones argued that computerisation was responsible for de-skilling. They also claim that many managerial and administrative jobs have become increasingly routine and are little different from clerical work. The post-industrial society thesis of Bell contradicts Braverman's ideas. He argues that white-collar and managerial positions will become more important because the revolution in IT and computers requires greater knowledge and technical understanding. Such workers will have greater control over their work.

> This question could have used the data in Item A to greater effect.

In conclusion, then, there is considerable disagreement whether emerging technologies are de-skilling clerical workers and middle management. The pessimistic outlook of Braverman is refuted by the more optimistic outlook of Bell. What is evident, however, is that unemployment in the service sector is increasing as the mega-mergers mentioned in Item A continue,

Sample question and model answer *(continued)*

especially at a global level. The recent crisis in the global financial
markets is likely to add to this.

f) **Assess sociological explanations for the ethnic differences in participation in the
labour market shown in Item B.** **[20 marks]**

f) If we examine the figures in Item B we can see that 86.1% of white men
aged between 16 and 64 were economically active. The numbers of ethnic
minorities who are economically active is lower, e.g. Afro-Caribbeans 80.4%,
Indians 80.8% and Pakistani/Bangladeshi 72.3%. This is possibly due to
ethnic minority youth being in FE/HE or on YTS and other training schemes.

The statistics for women show greater differences. For example, 71.9% of
white women were economically active compared with only 24.8% of
Pakistani/Bangladeshi women. This may reflect different cultural attitudes
towards womens' domestic role. For example, it is increasingly acceptable
amongst white women to combine career and motherhood. We can speculate
that this is less acceptable in some communities.

Jones explains employment differences between ethnic males in terms of
education. He notes that whites, Indians and Chinese men are more likely
to have A Levels and above than Afro-Caribbean and Pakistani/Bangladeshi
men. Jones does note that upward social mobility has improved for Indian
and Afro-Caribbean men but the latter group were still less than half as
likely than white men to get top jobs.

Murray claims that increasing numbers of young blacks are unwilling to
work and have become dependent upon welfare benefits. The Weberian
sociologists, Rex and Tomlinson argue that ethnic minorities and women are
to be found as a disproportionate part of the secondary labour market in
which jobs are low paid, insecure and characterised by poor conditions and
opportunities. Brown argues that these racial disadvantages in the labour
market are the result of racism and the prejudice of employers. His study
made bogus applications for jobs by letter and telephone using ethnic names
and accents. They found that white applicants, despite having the same
qualifications and experiences, were more likely to receive positive responses
from employers.

Marxists argue that ethnic minorities and women are part of a reserve
army of labour which is hired in times of economic boom and fired in
times of economic recession. Castles and Kosack argue that the existence
of such a group helps maintain the inequality of capitalist society because
ethnic minorities can be used to socially control white workers – demands
for higher wages or to explain the unemployment of white workers. For
example, ethnic minorities can be blamed for taking white workers' jobs,
thus diverting attention away from the deficiencies of capitalism.

However, to conclude, both Weberian and Marxist accounts have been
accused of over-simplifying the issue. Miles notes that some ethnic
minority members occupy very good jobs while some whites occupy very poor
jobs or are unemployed. It is therefore too simplistic to assume that there
is a sharp dividing line between ethnic minorities and the white majority.

Practice examination questions

Item A

In the 20th century, factory work has been dominated by the 'scientific management' theory of Frederick Taylor. His idea was to divide work into smaller and smaller repetitive units. Assembly-line production is a good example of this technique. However, although it increased production enormously, it also led to major dissatisfaction at work and a history of industrial action in areas of industry such as car manufacturing.

Item B

Work is a central and essential activity in many people's lives. The amount of job satisfaction we derive from work is a significant contributor to our sense of purpose and self-esteem. However, Marxists argue that the organisation of capitalism has taken creative opportunities away from workers. Instead, workers are slaves of machines and management practices which result in them having little or no control over the work process. Marxists argue that workers therefore experience alienation. They cannot identify with their work or the finished product. They feel indifferent, sometimes even hostile, to it. Blauner, on the other hand, rejects this argument. He argues that satisfaction, and therefore alienation, varies according to the technology used in a particular industry.

1   Explain what is meant by scientific management.   [2 marks]

2   Identify and briefly illustrate two types of industrial action.   [4 marks]

3   Suggest three ways in which Taylorism may have reduced job satisfaction.   [6 marks]

4   Identify and discuss two reasons why industrial action statistics may not be an accurate reflection of this phenomena.   [8 marks]

5   Using material from Item A and elsewhere, critically evaluate theories of industrial action.   [20 marks]

6   Using both Items and other sources, assess the view that alienation varies according to the technology used in a particular industry.   [20 marks]

Chapter 10

Health

The following topics are covered in this chapter:

- Definitions of health and illness
- Inequalities in health care
- The organisation of health care

10.1 Definitions of health and illness

LEARNING SUMMARY

After studying this section you should be able to:

- identify how health and illness are social as well as biological constructs
- distinguish between different approaches to mental health and illness

The social construction of illness

AQA ▶ U1

> **KEY POINT**
>
> **Roger Gomm** suggests that there is more to illness, disease, pain, etc. than the experience of physical symptoms, i.e. subjective feelings of being 'unwell'. In modern societies, physical symptoms are only defined as illness, etc., when officially recognised by medical professionals using objective scientific diagnosis. Gomm argues definitions of health and illness are thus socially constructed in modern societies by a biomedical élite, i.e. doctors.

Health professionals have not always dominated definitions of health and illness, e.g. mental illness in the 16th century was often defined as possession by evil spirits, whilst in the 18th century it was seen as caused by moral weakness. Sexual diseases such as AIDS are today still regarded by some as being caused by immoral behaviour.

The biomedical model of health

The model subscribed to by health professionals.

Nicky Hart notes that the **bio-medical model** became influential in the late 19th century and became dominant with the setting up of the NHS in 1946. She notes that this model has six characteristics:

- It concentrates on the organic or **physical symptoms** of disease, e.g. schizophrenia is linked to chemical changes in the brain.
- **Doctors** are portrayed as the only people who have the necessary skills to identify symptoms of illness.
- It is **cure-oriented** and stresses treatments such as surgery, drugs, etc.
- Illness is seen as a **temporary** affair. Germs, etc., are identified and driven off by medical expertise.
- The individual is the site of the disease. The causes of disease are rarely located in the environment that the individual occupies.
- Treatment is best located in a **medical environment**, i.e. hospital rather than in the environment where the symptoms may have arisen.

Alternative or holistic medicine is critical of the biomedical neglect of the relationship between the body and the mind, or the person and his/her immediate environment.

The social model of health

McKeown is worth knowing in detail.

> **KEY POINT**
>
> **McKeown** points out that health levels as measured by increases in life expectancy and decreases in child mortality had dramatically improved before the development of modern biomedical techniques such as vaccination. McKeown argues that 19th century public-health measures, e.g. sewage systems, clean water supplies, etc., improvements in nutrition and diet, and birth limitation are mainly responsible for good health today.

Gomm notes powerful groups have used medicine to control the behaviour of less powerful groups. In the USA homosexuality was officially classed as a mental illness until the 1980s. Illnesses may therefore be constructed in order to control 'problem' groups.

In conclusion, definitions of health and illness are not fixed or universal. Rather, they are subjected to constant change because they are socially constructed rather than biologically determined.

Mental health and illness

 U1

Some types of mental disorder are obviously physiological, e.g. Alzheimer's disease. However, there has long been a debate about whether such illnesses as depression or schizophrenia are physiological, e.g. caused by chemical imbalances in the brain.

Henshaw and Howells (1999) define mental illness as behaviour preventing individuals functioning adequately in their society. However, 'functioning adequately' may be dependent upon interpretation by powerful groups – e.g. dissidents in the former USSR were interpreted as 'mentally ill' and treated in psychiatric units. Sociologists therefore argue that mental illness is partly socially constructed.

Labelling theory and mental health

Labelling theory, in particular, has challenged non-sociological approaches. Both **Scheff (1966)** and **Szasz** have claimed that mental illness is merely a label applied to the behaviour of certain people at certain times and in certain situations – i.e. what is 'normal' or 'mad' behaviour is a matter of interpretation. Moreover, definitions of behaviour are relative – they vary over historical periods and across societies.

Scheff argued that there was no such thing as mental illness. Szasz argues that it is merely a means of socially controlling objectionable behaviour. Szasz also argues that such labels are confusing, e.g. the label of 'clinical depression' may disguise the fact that someone is very miserable for good reason.

Institutionalisation and mental health

Goffman (1968) claims that there is great stigma attached to mental illness in Western society and so societal reaction to the label is likely to be negative. Labelling and the consequent treatment by mental health professionals can result in a 'deviant career', i.e. those labelled accept the definition of themselves as 'ill'.

Goffman is particularly critical of the role of psychiatric hospitals in this process. His observations of patients suggest that such institutions attempt to make patients conform to institutional labels by stripping them of their old identities – what he calls 'mortification of self'. Institutional life involves learning to conform to the new role of 'mentally ill' as defined by psychiatric workers. **Rosenhan's (1975)** pseudo-patient experiment showed that staff rarely challenge the label of 'mentally ill' and consequently all behaviour, however normal, is interpreted in the context of mental illness.

> The film 'One Flew Over the Cuckoo's Nest' contains good examples of these responses.

KEY POINT

Goffman notes that patients respond in a variety of ways to this labelling. Some will withdraw, i.e. become introverted; others will rebel but be subjected to harsher treatment for their trouble. Some patients co-operate with staff, while others become dependent upon their labels, i.e. institutionalised. Others 'play it cool' and attempt to avoid trouble.

Goffman's case-study was a useful insight into institutionalisation despite being too small to generalise from. However, he has been criticised by both Marxists and feminists for neglecting influences on mental illness such as poverty and patriarchy.

Community care

> Read the newspapers and work out what the current political response is to community care for the mentally ill.

Today institutionalisation is less likely in the UK because in the 1980s many large mental hospitals were closed down and replaced by 'community care'. People were either treated at home or they were placed in accommodation and treated in day-care centres. The aims of community care were threefold:

- to avoid the problems of institutionalisation
- to avoid marginalising the mentally ill. It was hoped that they would be treated as normal members of the community
- to save money – institutional care is expensive.

However, two major problems have been perceived over the last ten years with community care:

- There is public concern that the release of psychiatric patients into the community puts 'ordinary' people at risk.
- The policy has not been properly organised or funded, e.g. in some areas ex-patients receive insufficient support in terms of hostels and trained staff available.

Progress check

1 What is biomedicine?

2 How was mental illness explained before the 20th century?

3 What three factors does McKeown argue are responsible for better health?

4 What, according to Scheff and Szasz, is mental illness?

5 What is a deviant career?

6 What is the relationship between community care and institutionalisation?

6 One of the main objectives of care in the community was to avoid the negative consequences of incarceration in homes and hospitals.
5 People labelled as mentally ill may come to see themselves as such.
4 A label applied by society to people whose behaviour is regarded as different or threatening.
3 Public health schemes, diet and contraception.
2 As either demonic possession or moral weakness.
1 An approach to health dominated by a medical élite which defines illness as being determined by biological or physical factors.

10.2 Inequalities in health care

After studying this section you should be able to:

- *identify trends in the social distribution of health and illness in regard to social class, gender and ethnicity*
- *outline and assess different explanations of inequalities in the provision of, and access to, health care*

LEARNING SUMMARY

The social distribution of health and illness

AQA   U1

If health and illness were chance occurrences we could expect to see them randomly distributed across the population. However, we can see that some groups can expect an over-proportionate amount of illness.

- The working class experience poorer mortality and morbidity rates than the middle classes, e.g. more than 3500 working-class babies would survive per year if the working-class infant mortality rate was reduced to middle-class levels.

- The working class are also more likely to die pre-retirement of cancer, stroke and heart disease than the middle class.

Cultural deprivation theory

Blaming the victim!

> This theory argues that inequalities in health between the working class and middle class are the product of culture. Working-class culture is seen to be composed of values which are harmful to health.

KEY POINT

Cultural deprivationists suggest that the working class are less likely to eat a healthy diet and more likely to smoke and drink excessively. **Roberts** argues that the working class indulge in less exercise and are more passive in terms of their leisure pursuits. Cultural deprivationists have also suggested that the working class are less likely to take advantage of preventative health care, vaccination or ante-natal care. **Ann Howlett and John Ashley** suggest that the middle class have more knowledge of what constitutes good health than the working class. Consequently the middle class attempt to prevent health problems through exercise and diet.

Critics of cultural deprivation theory argue that:

> - cultural values may be a realistic response to the poverty and material deprivation caused by unemployment and/or low wages. Cost may be the major reason why working-class people do not subscribe to healthy diets, exercise and take-up of NHS facilities. They may be well aware of the benefits of these but unable to afford them. Smoking and drinking may be an attempt to relieve stress.

KEY POINT

- Moreover, the working class take-up of NHS facilities may have little to do with poor attitudes. Research by **Cartwright and O'Brien** suggests that working-class patients feel intimidated by the middle-class nature of health care. They found that doctors spend much more time with middle-class patients and know far more about them than working-class patients.

The social administration theory

Blaming government policy.

This view argues that health inequalities are largely caused by inequalities in the distribution of NHS resources.

> KEY POINT
>
> • Tudor Hart (1971) suggests that the allocation of NHS resources is so unequal that it conforms to an 'inverse care law' – a law which states that those whose need is less get more health resources whilst those in greatest need get less. Working-class areas tend to be provided with the fewest and worse health facilities in terms of numbers of GPs and hospitals.

However, in criticism of the Social Administration model, the healthiest part of the UK (i.e. East Anglia), has never received a fair share of funding, whilst Scotland has always received more funding than England and Wales. Tudor Hart's criticisms may also have dated. The NHS underwent tremendous organisational change, especially in the period 1979–97.

Marxism

Blaming capitalism.

Marxist sociologists suggest that in capitalist societies it is inevitable that health will become a market commodity like any other. Marxists suggest that government cutbacks in health spending in the 1980s were aimed at encouraging people to turn to private health care. The ability to pay for health clearly benefits some groups at the expense of others.

The Marxists, Doyal and Pennell, note that the fundamental purpose of capitalism is the pursuit of profit. They suggest that this has three negative consequences for the health of the working classes.

> KEY POINT
>
> • Less attention is paid to the welfare of workers, e.g. approximately 700 workers are killed in industrial accidents every year in the UK, whilst death from industrial disease is also common.
>
> • Jobs are not only physically dangerous but also psychologically dangerous. The demands of repetitive and de-skilled work performed at high speed, combined with increased rates of overtime and shift work, result in stress.
>
> • Employers have a vested interest in keeping wages at a low level in order to maximise profits. This may result in poverty. Two Government-sponsored reports, The Black Report (1980) and The Health Divide (1987) identify the chief causes of ill health amongst the working class as poverty. Townsend and Phillimore (1986), in a study of health in the North East, note the relationship between bad housing, poor diet, lack of play areas, overcrowding, poor education and exposure to infection. They conclude 'the health gap is a consequence of the wealth gap'.

Marxists suggest that the biomedical model of health plays an ideological role in that it directs attention away from the real causes of disease, such as material deprivation and the nature of work in capitalist society.

However, Nicky Hart accuses Doyal and Pennell of being selective in their use of evidence. She notes that they fail to acknowledge that many of the commodities and medical technologies of advanced capitalist society are very beneficial to health. Moreover, the former socialist countries of Eastern Europe probably experience worse health levels than the West. Hart concludes that poor health is linked to industrialisation rather than its organisation along capitalist or socialist lines.

Gender and health

A number of differences in mortality and morbidity can be perceived between men and women.

- Women tend to live longer than men in all social classes. Life expectancy at birth in the UK is 77 years for females but 71 for males.

- Women experience more chronic sickness (i.e. long-standing illness, disability or infirmity) than men. Two-thirds of the four million disabled people in the UK are women.

- Women are more likely to suffer from emotional disturbance, depression and acute stress than men – and are much more likely to be receiving drug treatment for such problems.

- Women see their doctor more frequently than men.

Explanations for gender inequalities

Alison McFarlane suggests that the statistics are misleading. She notes that once visits to the GP in connection with contraception, menstruation, gynaecology and post-natal care are taken into consideration the differences between males and females disappear.

However, it is still a fact that more women are treated for mental health problems and degenerative diseases. The latter is probably due to the fact that women are more likely than men to survive beyond retirement age.

Gender role socialisation

This is seen by some liberal feminists as the reason for differences in mortality and morbidity rates because:

> This material is also quite useful in supporting the gender-role socialisation material in Chapter 4.

• Men are socialised into being more aggressive and into taking more risks. This could account for the high death rate for males aged between 15 and 35. Many of these deaths result from acts of violence and motor accidents.
• It is more acceptable for men to smoke and drink alcohol, which may account for the higher rate of death from cancer and heart disease in the 45–55 age group.
• Men are expected to be breadwinners in our culture. Therefore they are more likely to be victims of industrial accidents, disease and stress. They are more likely to suffer the stress of unemployment.

KEY POINT

> Link to family

Some feminists have also contributed to this gender role socialisation argument by focusing on the mother–housewife role. Ann Oakley's (1976) interviews with working-class and middle-class housewives discovered that they experienced housework as both monotonous and isolated. Jesse Bernard argues that marriage makes women sick. She found that married men have better mental and physical health than single men but this position is reversed with married and single women.

Labelling theory

Busfield (1983) notes that the diagnosis of mental illness in women may reflect negative stereotypes held by doctors about female behaviour. Certain types of behaviour, e.g. being angry, shouting, etc., may be labelled as illness (e.g. hysteria) because they do not fit conventional perceptions of femininity. Consequently, what is labelled overwork in men may be labelled as depression in women.

Marxist feminists argue that the labelling of some women as mentally ill has an ideological function because it ignores women's domestic environment which is the real cause of the problem.

> **Radical feminists** would conclude that the NHS is a patriarchal institution, e.g. they note that 75% of NHS workers are female. However, despite the fact that nearly 25% of hospital doctors are female, only 14% are consultants and only 15% are GPs. Almost 90% of nurses are female, as are 73% of chiropodists, 89% of dieticians and occupational therapists, and 86% of physiotherapists.
>
> **KEY POINT**

The social control of women's health

Radical feminists also suggest that males socially construct definitions of health and illness. For example:

- Both the pill and IUDs carry significant health risks which men would not be expected to tolerate.
- Control over childbirth has been taken away from women. Pregnancy is seen as an 'illness' and pregnant women are viewed as patients.
- Aspects of women's health such as post-natal depression, menstruation and the menopause have been neglected by biomedicine.

Ethnicity and health

AQA ▶ U1

A number of trends can be seen in regard to ethnicity and health in the UK:

- Asians and Afro-Caribbeans suffer higher than average levels of liver cancer, diabetes, tuberculosis and high blood pressure.
- Asian children are more likely to suffer from rickets.
- Admission rates to psychiatric hospitals for Afro-Caribbeans, especially Rastafarians, are higher than average.

There are various theories that provide explanations for ethnic inequalities.

Cultural deprivation theory

Blaming the victims.

This theory focuses on health-damaging behaviour which allegedly is caused by the cultural or religious beliefs of ethnic minorities. It is suggested that:

- the Asian diet (especially the use of ghee fat and the alleged high carbohydrate content of food) is unhealthy.
- Immigrant groups experience 'language difficulties' and this is responsible for their failure to use NHS facilities.

However, Marmot (1984) suggests that such lifestyle factors play only a minor role. He argues:

- Asian diets are arguably closer to health education advice on low-fat diets than the traditional British diet.
- Language should not be a problem as the numbers of British-born ethnic minorities increases.

Social administration theory

Blaming health policy.

This view of health is critical of the NHS's treatment of ethnic minorities and suggests that ethnic minorities are likely to experience unequal access to health services because:

KEY POINT

- their needs are often unrecognised or ignored, and consequently ethnic-minority groups may find vital provision irrelevant, offensive, unhelpful or threatening (Mares, 1987)
- NHS facilities may fail to provide health information in the appropriate language
- NHS facilities may fail to make knowledge of religious, dietary and cultural norms basic to health professional training
- NHS facilities may fail to provide amenities which support cultural beliefs such as the importance of, for example, prayer in hospital, death rites, etc.

The Marxist view

Blaming capitalism.

Marxists argue that it is important to consider the location of the black population in the class structure. Ethnic minorities are more likely to be:

- concentrated in low-paid, manual occupations and particularly in industries that are most hazardous to health
- subjected to the stresses of unemployment and lack of job security
- subjected to the stresses of shift work
- located in poor-quality, overcrowded housing and sharing bathroom/toilets.

Blaming racism.

Such problems will be compounded by **racism**. **Brown** suggests that racist practices by employers and landlords mean that ethnic minorities are more likely to face these problems than whites in poverty. Racism may also have a more direct impact in the form of racial attacks.

Some commentators have suggested that the large number of Rastafarians in the mental-health system may be the result of the British justice system's labelling of this group. They may be defined as a problem because their behaviour does not conform to the 'norm'.

Don't neglect class and gender.

It is important to note that race interacts with other important social factors especially social class and gender, e.g. some Asian groups (notably East African Asian), tend to occupy higher social-class positions than other Asian groups and consequently enjoy health levels similar to the white middle class. Ethnic-minority women may experience worse health than ethnic-minority men, according to **Blackburn (1991)**.

Progress check

1 What does cultural deprivation theory blame for inequalities in health?
2 What do material deprivationists blame for inequalities in health?
3 What is the 'inverse care law'?
4 What do Marxists claim is the major cause of ill health?
5 What female social role is blamed by Oakley, Bernard and Graham for the poor health of women?
6 What sociological explanation has been given for the large numbers of Afro-Caribbean people in the mental health system?

6 Racist labelling in the criminal justice system.
5 The mother–housewife role.
4 Capitalism.
3 Those whose need is less get more health resources, whilst those in greatest need get less.
2 Poverty.
1 The cultural habits of the poor.

10.3 The organisation of health care

After studying this section you should be able to:

- *outline and assess different explanations of the role of medicine and the health professions*
- *identify recent changes in the organisation of health care in the UK*

Health, professionals and social control

AQA ▷ U1

Doctors as public servants.

Functionalism, medical professionals and altruism

Functionalists see the medical profession as primarily altruistic. Doctors serve the public interest rather than pursue private gain. The Hippocratic oath is indicative of this social commitment – doctors swear to do all they can to help the sick regardless of material interest.

Functionalists also see medicine as important as an **agency of social control**. They argue that social order depends upon value consensus and the inter-dependence of skills. Illness disrupts the industrial system because it involves people dropping out to recuperate. People may use illness as an excuse to withdraw from their social obligations. In this sense, illness is deviant and must be socially controlled.

> **Parsons** argues that the power of doctors is used in the interests of society. Doctors officially confirm the 'sick role' and thus sanction the withdrawal of people from the economy. The doctor's social-control role is thus to maintain social responsibility amongst the ill and to encourage their swift return to their social roles.

KEY POINT

However, functionalism has been subjected to the following criticisms.

- Its analysis tends to neglect **private medicine** – the existence of which challenges the idea that the medical profession is primarily altruistic.
- Hart also notes that if altruism were the primary motivation of doctors, the NHS would devote more resources to **disease prevention** than it currently does.
- Parsons' sick role theory suggests that ill people are passive social actors who obey the demands of doctors without question. Evidence from **Cartwright** suggests that conflict between doctors and patients is the norm.

Marxism, medical professionals and ideological control

Marxists generally see medicine as a **social institution which supports capitalist interests**. They suggest that the power of doctors is not geared to altruism, but rather, it functions to reproduce class inequality.

Doctors as agents of
social control.

> **Doyal** sees doctors as performing a **conservative social function**. Marxists argue that doctors and the NHS are part of an **ideological state apparatus** working on behalf of the capitalist class to reproduce and legitimate class inequality. The role of doctors therefore is to:
> - maintain the health and productivity of the workforce
> - validate, or otherwise, the claims of workers to have time off work; Doctors therefore prevent workers from dropping out of the system and thus minimise disruption to the capitalist system
> - obscure the real causes of disease such as class inequality and exploitation caused by capitalism (e;g. poverty, low wages, etc.) by blaming the sick for their illness or by suggesting that illness is a random phenomenon.

K E Y P O I N T

Marxists such as **Doyal** argue that in return for performing this ideological function doctors are rewarded with status, high financial rewards and monopoly over medical knowledge. The power of doctors is therefore granted to them by the capitalist class in return for acting as agents of social control.

Medical professionals and occupational strategies

Doctors as self-serving
professionals.

The **Weberian sociologist, Friedson** points out that the medical profession has achieved a legal monopoly over health in the UK. The British Medical Association controls recruitment, training and practice and regulates professional conduct. Only doctors have a legal right to diagnose and treat illness. They also have a major say in the running of the NHS. In return, the medical profession is supposed to guarantee high ethical standards. Doctors appear to the public as a standard product, equally skilful and equally trustworthy, i.e. as altruistic.

> Friedson argues that the basis of professional power is **legal – rational** rather than economic. Doctors are socially autonomous of the capitalist class. Friedson is also sceptical of the **altruistic** role of doctors. He notes that medical power is mainly aimed at serving the interests of doctors. It is an **occupational strategy** that has ensured high financial rewards.

K E Y P O I N T

The National Health Service

AQA   1.23

The National Health Service was set up in 1948 by the Labour Government in order to create a system of universal and free health care. Both Labour and Conservative governments subscribed to a **consensus** about how the NHS should be run until 1979, when Mrs Thatcher took power.

Conservative reform of the NHS

This has focused on four key areas.

- The principles of the **free market** (such as competition) were introduced to health care. An **internal market** was created. GPs became responsible for their own budgets (**fundholders**). They could purchase services from hospital trusts on behalf of patients registered to them. The idea was that competition would promote efficiency and reduce costs as trusts competed with each other to provide services. Managers were recruited from business to oversee this system.
- **Care in the community** was designed to take the old, sick, disabled and mentally ill out of institutional care and back into the care of family and the wider community.

Contrast with New Labour.

- Private health schemes and hospitals were encouraged. This period also saw an expansion of private homes for the elderly.
- A Patient's Charter was introduced in 1992 in order to make clear what performance standards the health service was supposed to achieve.

Criticism of conservative reforms suggests the health service has been transformed into a three-tier service which merely reproduces the inverse care law:

- The wealthy have access to a private health-care system.
- The middle class are registered with GPs in rural or suburban practices in which demand on funds is not so great. This gives GPs more choice of services.
- Working-class patients tend to be registered to GPs in inner cities who face intensive demands on their funds. They therefore have less flexibility in how they spend their funds.

New Labour and the NHS

Contrast with Conservative reforms.

The Labour Government experienced a crisis in its handling of the NHS in January 2000. It was noted that the UK has fewer doctors and hospital beds than almost any other country in Europe per head of population. However, Labour intends to:

- abolish the internal market
- raise health expenditure to the European average by 2002
- set up Primary care trusts – autonomous, statutory bodies run by GPs, nurses and other health professionals, handling annual budgets of at least £60m. They will offer services such as high street health centres.
- put more emphasis on preventative health care
- focus on the relationship between health, poverty, housing, environment and lifestyle
- reduce waiting lists.

Progress check

1 What does altruism mean?
2 What sociological theory claims that doctors are altruistic?
3 What is the 'sick role'?
4 How do Marxists view doctors?
5 Why does Friedson reject the view that doctors are altruistic?
6 What is the 'internal market' in the NHS?

6 Competition between providers of heath care (e.g. hospital trusts) to provide services to purchasers such as fundholding GPs.
5 Because control over medicine is an occupational strategy aimed at ensuring high status and rewards.
4 As ideological agents of capitalism.
3 The obligation of sick members of society to attempt to return to their social obligations as quickly as possible by consulting doctors.
2 Functionalism.
1 Working primarily for the public good.

Sample question and model answer

A typical AQA question.

You will have 1 hour and 15 minutes. Spend 15 minutes reading the data and planning your response.

Item A

We need to look carefully at the processes whereby someone is categorised as being mentally ill. What kinds of behaviour are deemed to be normal, socially acceptable, whilst others are not? What levels of intellectual functioning are necessary to enable the individual to be regarded as a fully competent member of society? What sorts of people typically fall into these categories?

When we look at a range of societies, and when we look back over time, we can clearly see that there are no simple or uniform answers to these questions. In the past we tolerated and accommodated 'the village idiot'. If someone was a bit eccentric or behaved unpredictably, we knew to give them a wide berth, but nothing more. Now, we have to intervene and treat everyone, seemingly to make them conform to a very specific model of conformity.

Extracted from P. Stephens et al., Think Sociology, *Stanley Thorne, 1998*

Item B

1 hour should be spent writing.

Inequalities in health (as measured by morbidity and mortality rates) exist in all Western European countries. Health inequalities mirror class inequalities (income and job opportunities) and countries with less class division in general have higher life expectancies. Those in manual occupations have higher mortality rates on average than the non-manual workers. In terms of morbidity there are also clear differences: the unemployed, those in lowly paid occupations and those who are very poorly educated are more likely to suffer from chronic illness than other groups in the population. Unskilled and skilled workers are more likely to take sick leave and are more likely to receive hospital care than higher civil servants and salaried employees.

Adapted from T. Spybey (ed.), Britain in Europe: An Introduction to Sociology, *Routledge, 1997*

Don't over-respond to questions a–d in terms of time spent and length.

a) Explain what is meant by 'morbidity'. [2 marks]

a) Morbidity refers to ill health resulting from disease.

b) Identify two historical reasons for mental illness before it was defined as a medical problem. [4 marks]

b) Moral weakness.
Possession by spirits or demons.

c) Using Item B only, suggest three ways in which 'health inequalities mirror class inequalities'. [6 marks]

c) Any three from:

Non-manual workers have longer life expectancy than manual workers.

The unemployed, the low paid and the poorly educated are more likely to experience chronic illness than any other social group.

Unskilled and skilled workers are more likely to be admitted to hospital than civil servants.

Unskilled workers are more likely to be on sick leave than white-collar workers (i.e. salaried employees).

Sample question and model answer *(continued)*

d) Identify and briefly describe two criticisms of the care in the community mental health programme. **[8 marks]**

d) Two from:

Community care for the mentally ill underestimated the care and security required for some patients who would otherwise have been locked up in secure hospitals. In reaction to this, New Labour has announced improvements in supervision of patients causing concern.

Stephen Moore notes that the original costing for community care suggested that it would cost less than institutional care. However, it has been more expensive to have services spread across personal and health services. Yet community care has been under-funded and there is suspicion that the closing of hospitals was essentially a cost-cutting exercise. Much of the £2000 million saved was not re-directed back into the community care programme.

e) Explain why some sociologists believe that mental illness is a product of social categories rather than physical or biological factors. **[20 marks]**

> Spend 20 minutes on this.

e) Some types of mental disorder are obviously biological or physiological, e.g. Alzheimer's disease. However, Henshaw and Howells (1999) define mental illness as behaviour preventing individuals functioning adequately in their society. However, they point out that 'functioning adequately' may be dependent upon interpretation by powerful groups. For example, dissidents in the former USSR were interpreted as 'mentally ill' and treated in psychiatric units. Sociologists therefore argue that mental illness is partly socially constructed. Both Scheff (1966) and Szasz have claimed what is 'normal' or 'mad' behaviour is a matter of interpretation. Definitions of behaviour are also relative – they vary over historical period and across societies. For example, behaviour which is regarded as eccentric in the

> Note use of Item A.

past may be likely to be defined as disturbed today. As Item A suggests, we simply tolerated and accommodated the village idiot in the past. If someone was a bit strange, we simply avoided them. Today the 'odd' and 'eccentric' are more likely to be treated. Szasz argues that definitions of mental illness are simply means of controlling behaviour that is seen as objectionable by powerful groups. As Item A states, intervention means making people conform to a very specific model of conformity. Busfield (1983) notes that the diagnosis of mental illness in women may reflect

> Note question is asking for exploration – no evaluation is called for.

negative stereotypes held by doctors about female behaviour. Similarly, some commentators have suggested that the large number of Rastafarians in the mental-health system may be the result of the British justice system's labelling of this group. They may be defined as a problem because their behaviour does not conform to the 'norm'.

Goffman (1968) claims that there is great stigma attached to mental illness in Western society. Consequently, societal reaction to the label is likely to be negative. Goffman is particularly critical of the role of psychiatric hospitals. His observations of patients suggest that such institutions attempt to make patients conform to institutional labels by stripping them of their old identities. Goffman calls this process 'mortification of self'. Institutional life involves learning to conform to the new role of 'mentally ill' as defined by psychiatric workers.

Sample question and model answer *(continued)*

Today, institutionalisation is less likely in the UK because in the 1980s many large mental hospitals were closed down and replaced by 'community care'. People were either treated at home or they were placed in accommodation and treated in day-care centres.

20 minutes should be spent on this.

f) Using material from Item B, and elsewhere, assess explanations for class inequalities in health. **[20 marks]**

Note emphasis on Item B.

f) If health and illness were chance occurrences we could expect to see them randomly distributed across the population. However, this is not the case – rather we can see from Item B that some groups can expect an over-proportionate amount of illness. The working class experience poorer mortality and morbidity rates than the middle classes.

This response evaluates by contrasting theories but also explicitly criticises the specifics of particular theories.

Sociologists have attempted to explain these social variations in morbidity and mortality. Cultural deprivationists argue that working-class people lead unhealthy lifestyles in terms of smoking and diet. They also suggest that lack of education may mean the working class are less likely to take advantage of NHS facilities, especially visiting the doctor and preventative medicine.

However, this theory has been criticised for neglecting the economic circumstances of this group. For example, poverty may be the cause of poor diet rather than lack of education.

The Social Administration view argues that health inequalities are largely caused by inequalities in the distribution of NHS resources. Tudor Hart (1971) suggests that the allocation of NHS resources is so unequal that it conforms to an 'inverse care law'. This law states that those whose need is less get more health resources, whilst those in greatest need get less. Working-class areas tend to be provided with the fewest and worse health facilities in terms of numbers of GPs and hospitals. However, Tudor Hart's criticisms may have dated. The NHS has undergone tremendous organisational change since 1971.

Item B could have been used to a fuller extent.

Marxists such as Doyal and Pennell link ill health specifically to capitalism's pursuit of profit which they claim means less attention is paid to the welfare of workers. For example, approximately 700 people are killed at work annually. Marxists also note a strong link between low wages, unemployment, poor housing, etc. and poor health. As Item B notes, health inequalities reflect class inequalities in income and job opportunities. Countries with less social class divisions experience less health inequalities.

However, critics note that capitalism has dramatically improved the life expectancy of all sections of society. However, it is important to remember that the mortality gap between the middle class and working class has actually increased since 1979.

Practice examination questions

Item A

The major causes of death in 19th-century Britain were infectious diseases such as tuberculosis and smallpox. However, by the end of this century, such diseases were in decline. It is widely believed that biomedical advances were responsible for improvements in infant mortality and the increase in life expectancy experienced in this period. However, McKeown (1979) has challenged this view. He shows that death from such diseases were long in decline before the introduction of effective medical treatment such as vaccinations. McKeown argues that people became more resistant to disease because of better nutrition, improved public-health conditions (especially the introduction of clean piped water, sewage disposal systems and toilets) and changes in personal behaviour such as increased use of contraception and better personal hygiene.

Item B

Health is a major issue of concern to women. Women form the majority of workers in the health service and are, in the family, responsible for the health of others. However, until the development of feminist sociology, little attention was paid to the influence of gender on health. Feminists pointed out that the multiple roles that women play affect their physical and mental well-being. However, most research into work and ill health has focused on male-dominated occupations. Little attention has been paid to the health hazards where women predominate, and even less to those of the housewife.

Adapted from P. Abbott and C. Wallace, An Introduction to Sociology: Feminist Perspectives, Routledge, 1990

1   Explain what sociologists mean by 'infant mortality'.   [2 marks]

2   Identify two roles that women may play that may affect their physical and mental well-being. (Item B)   [4 marks]

3   Suggest three ways in which biomedicine has improved health during the course of the 20th century.   [6 marks]

4   Identify and briefly describe two feminist criticisms of the patriarchal nature of the medical profession.   [8 marks]

5   Explain the view that improved life expectancy in the UK has little to do with medical advances.   [20 marks]

6   Using material from Item B and elsewhere, evaluate explanations for gender inequalities in mortality and morbidity.   [20 marks]

Practice examination answers

Chapter 1 Research methods

This is a typical OCR Research Methods question.

1 Note the emphasis on the word 'briefly'. Validity refers to whether the data collected actually reflects the social reality of whatever the sociologist is studying. It is always a good idea to include an example to illustrate your definition.

2 There are three aspects to the design. Take each in turn.

- Will the schools co-operate considering the subject of the research? Will their co-operation vary depending on whether they are state or private? If so, why? How do you overcome these problems?

- Will students volunteer for such a study? Think about the potential problems of interview bias caused by the fact that the teachers will be the interviewers and the interviews will be conducted in class-time.

- Think about the general weaknesses of structured interviews. How might they apply in this situation?

3 There are not a great deal of marks available for this question but it's worth attempting to make at least four observations. For example:

- Over a third of 14 year olds have tried drugs and this increases to over half of 15 year olds.

- However, drug taking does not look as if it is a regular affair for the majority of teenagers in the 14–16 range. Only one-fifth of 14-year-olds had used drugs in the past month, although this increases to 28% for fifteen-year-olds.

- The age range 14–16 looks like the period when experimentation with drugs is most likely to take place. For example, 41% of fifteen-year-olds and 41% of sixteen-year-olds had used drugs in the past year.

- On the whole, however, apart from fifteen-year-olds, the majority of 14–16 year-olds had never used drugs.

4 Note that the emphasis is on knowledge and understanding (outline in detail) although some evaluation is necessary (briefly assess). The data has already referred to structured interviews. The type of method most suitable to the subject matter of young people's use of drugs is probably a self-report questionnaire and you should include the following points in your answer:

- the need to use a combination of open questions (to gather qualitative data in terms of attitudes, motives, etc.) and closed questions (to gather quantitative data such as when, how long, how many, etc.);

- stress anonymity and confidentiality

- use school registers as sampling frame. Randomly sample school population

- pilot interviews with pupils to provide ideas for questions plus add validity

- strengths of questionnaires: cheap, easy to distribute, bulk returned quickly

- weaknesses of questionnaires: inflexible, no possibility of probing in more depth, non-response (although anonymity, confidentiality and fact that questions are based on student experience should overcome this problem), exaggeration, distortion of experience, etc.

- follow up with unstructured interviews with willing participants to add more qualitative depth to the data collected by the questionnaire.

Chapter 2 The family

This is a typical OCR Family question.

1 Note the stress on 'explain'. You must illustrate whatever features of the reconstituted family (i.e. step-family) you decide to focus on which should be any two of:
- causes
- their relationship with other types of family
- potential tensions between family members.

2 This is worth 40 marks. Therefore it is worth writing at least two sides of A4. Before you can 'assess', you need to explain what is meant by 'dysfunctional'. Your plan therefore may look something like this:

- The number of one-parent families in the UK doubled from 12% of families in 1986 to 18% in 1994. Women (91%) head the great majority of single-parent families.

- Outline the New Right view, especially that of Murray. Other aspects worth mentioning include the economic costs of one-parent families, welfare dependency and alleged social-security fraud.

Assessment could focus on the following ideas:

- How the ideology of familism which stresses the nuclear family ideal has led to the negative labelling of one-parent families (see Chester, Popay, etc.). Illustrate with examples.

- How single parents have been scapegoated for social problems caused by structural factors such as unemployment, racism, the decline of the inner city, etc.

- Poverty: illustrate the problems faced by lone parents. Stress that these are hardly an incentive to choose this option.

- It is often preferable for a child to live with one caring parent than with parents who are in conflict with each other and who may scapegoat the child. See the work of Phoenix and Cashmore.

- However, conclude with a word of caution – children from one-parent families do less well in education than children from two-parent families, although we do not know what causes these differences. For example, it could be the lack of a father, poverty or the negative labels lone parents attract from politicians and the media.

Chapter 3 Education

This is a typical OCR Youth and Culture question focusing on education.

1 There are a number of possible responses to this:

- self-fulfilling prophecy (positive and negative)
- anti-school sub-culture (Hargreaves, Ball, Troyna, etc.)
- truancy
- resistance (Fuller, Willis, etc.).

2 Before you 'assess', outline and support the view that female under-achievement is a thing of the past.

- Begin by outlining the facts, i.e. female achievement dramatically improved throughout the 1980s and 1990s. Illustrate this with examples.

- Explain why girl-friendly educational practices were pursued in the 1980s. Illustrate with reference to (a) feminist research in the 1970s, (b) Girls into Science and Technology, (c) educational social policy, (d) the feminisation of the economy, and (e) the crisis of masculinity.

- Don't forget to assess. Single-sex schools serving middle-class catchment areas may be distorting the statistics. Working-class and black girls' success rates do not compare with white middle-class girls. Gender stereotyping continues in some subject areas. Despite the feminisation of the workforce, gender equality in pay and employment conditions does not exist.

Chapter 4 The individual and society

This is a typical OCR question.

1 Any two choices from:

- family life, e.g. distribution of household tasks
- leisure pursuits, e.g. football or rugby league rather than golf or squash
- voting behaviour, e.g. traditionally voted Labour.

2 Any two from the following. It is a good idea to illustrate with an example.

- The decline of traditional jobs.
- The decline of traditional working-class areas.
- The adoption of a more individualistic outlook which stresses the individual and family at the expense of community solidarity.
- The lack of a truly Socialist political party stressing community and class solidarity, etc.

3 There has been limited research into how the **upper class** construct their social identity. However, focus on:

- cultural capital, i.e. they learn distinct modes of language, mannerisms, attitudes and values which clearly distinguish them from the masses
- this process of socialisation is reinforced by kinship, public school and Oxbridge education, membership of clubs, etc.
- this lifestyle results in a well-developed self confidence and sense of difference and social superiority.

  Savage's (1992) research described three types of **middle-class** identity.

- Professionals who subscribed to an ascetic or intellectual identity. Illustrate.
- Managers subscribed to an instrumentalist identity in that they defined success in terms of their standard of living and leisure pursuits. Illustrate.

- Savage identified a young group of entrepreneurial types working in the City, the mass media and advertising. This group subscribed to a 'post-modern' identity and revolves around consumption.

4 Before you can assess, start by examining those studies which indicate that the working class had a strong sense of cultural identity and contrast with studies which suggest working-class cultural identity is on the decline. Fifty years ago, studies of working-class communities showed them to be coherent and stable.

- 'Family and Kinship in East London' by Wilmott and Young (1957) demonstrated a distinct working-class lifestyle in terms of extended family systems and mutual support. Lockwood's (1966) research found that many workers subscribed to a value system he called 'proletarian traditionalist'. Illustrate this.
- Wilmott and Young claimed in the 1970s that such working-class communities were in decline. Illustrate why.
- Lash and Urry suggest the 'de-centring of class identity' has continued into the 1980s because of economic changes. Illustrate.
- The emergence of a 'new working class'? Illustrate with reference to Goldthorpe and Lockwood's 'privatised instrumentalists' (i.e. affluent workers) and Ivor Crewe's work on voting behaviour.
- Modern studies such as Saunders (1990) focus on consumption cleavages. Illustrate.
- Focus briefly on the underclass thesis.
- Finish by discussing the debate between post-modernist views and its focus on consumption and lifestyle, and Marshall, who argues that social class is still important in the construction of working-class identity.

Chapter 5 Mass media

This is a typical AQA question.

1 Representation refers to stereotypes or dominant images of particular groups found in the media.

2 Item B provides clues to your possible response, which you should illustrate with examples. Any two from: deregulation of parts of the media; the privatising of public companies; mergers; take-overs of smaller media companies; the development of global technologies, etc.

3 Note that the question is merely asking you to 'identify' a representation. Possibilities include:

   • They may be portrayed as a number problem, e.g. immigrants.

   • They may be portrayed as a welfare problem.

   • They may be represented as a crime problem.

   • Ethnic-minority concerns may not be a given a serious airing.

   • Positive role models may over-state sport and music.

4 Note emphasis on 'briefly describe', so explain why you have chosen any two of the criticisms below:

   • Evidence tends to be anecdotal rather than scientific.

   • Journalists have a sense of social responsibility to the truth as symbolised by investigative reporting.

   • Some media organisations do not have an owner, e.g. they may be public organisations like the BBC.

   • Governments may prevent proprietor interference via laws.

5 The focus is on 'outlining' ideas rather than evaluating them. However, it is probably a good idea to contrast two views, i.e. that owners control the content of the media and that media professionals produce news objectively. Your plan might look something like this:

   • A brief outline of Miliband's ideas that the ownership and control of mass media is now in the hands of a small group of owners who manipulate news content. Briefly outline the evidence supporting Miliband, using concepts such as concentration and conglomeration.

   • General criticisms of Miliband? Evidence is anecdotal; even if media interference exists, does it affect the audience?

   • Outline the pluralist argument, particularly its stress on media personnel being objective professionals.

   • Outline the role of media professionals in the social construction of news, paying particular attention to the concept of news values.

   • Conclude with reference to hegemonic Marxists, i.e. news is the result of professional practices but tends to support the consensus and therefore be uncritical of the organisation of capitalist society.

6 Note that the question asks you to use information from Item A and other sources. Moreover, it asks for evaluation. Your plan should look like this:

   • Your introduction should identify the sociological source of the statement in the title, i.e. pluralism. It should also make clear that other theories, e.g. types of feminism, suggest that such gender stereotyping is still the norm.

   • Outline pluralist ideas in regard to media representations of gender.

   • Feminists identify continuing stereotyping – give examples, using Item A (e.g. women are predominantly portrayed as either mothers and housewives or as available for sex at any time) and other sources (e.g. women's issues not taken seriously). Support with quantitative data from studies such as Cumberbatch.

   • Outline the Radical feminist explanation for such stereotyping.

   • Evaluate using Barker (from Item A), liberal feminism (stereotyping is in decline) and socialist feminism (stereotyping is not a deliberate patriarchal policy – rather it is the product of commercial pressures).

Chapter 6 Religion

This is a typical OCR question.

1 Some religions do not allow women to lead religious services. Illustrate.

   Some religions ascribe the role of wife and mother to women as their primary function. Illustrate with reference to contraception.

2 Begin by explaining what is meant by 'disengaged from society' using Wilson's arguments, e.g. link to the concept of secularisation and illustrate using the view that the church is no longer involved in important areas of social life such as politics.

   • Outline supporting evidence – contrast with past attendance/membership figures; relationship between religion and past governments.

   • Outline conflicting evidence, i.e. assess – contemporary religion's role in education and welfare; continuing media interest in moral and religious matters; etc.

   • Outline other aspects of secularisation – religious pluralism; growth in number of sects, ecumenical movement, etc.

   • Outline arguments against religious pluralism, i.e. assess – see Greeley and G.K. Nelson.

   • Evaluative conclusion: how reliable and valid is the statistical evidence in favour of secularisation? No universal definition of religious belief and secularisation is shared by sociologists. Is secularisation a cyclical process? – see Stark and Bainbridge.

Chapter 7 Youth and culture

This is a typical OCR question.

1 Note the focus on 'explain'. Be willing to illustrate. There are a number of possibilities:

- labelling by teachers (see Becker, etc.)
- streaming (see Hargreaves)
- denial of status (see Albert Cohen)
- influence of working-class or ethnic-minority culture (see Paul Willis).

2 Begin by defining sub-culture, i.e. it refers to the existence of small groups with distinct identities and lifestyles which generally tend to be incompatible with mainstream culture. The major explanations which should be outlined and assessed include:

- Albert Cohen's theory of status frustration. Criticise using Willis.

- Walter Miller's 'focal concerns' theory. Criticise using Matza.
- Labelling theory. Focus especially on how young people are labelled via policing or media moral panics. Sub-cultures may be a form of resistance and compensation.
- Marxism – youth sub-cultures as a form of ideological resistance to the cultural dominance of the ruling class. Use the CCCS and Hebdige material. Criticise for neglecting the role of the media in constructing youth sub-cultures and for reading too much into sub-cultural style.
- The Left Realists, Lea and Young – criminal sub-cultures are a product of young people's interpretations of their position as relatively deprived and marginalised. However, this theory offers little empirical evidence for these assertions.

Chapter 8 Wealth, welfare and poverty

This is a typical AQA question.

1 Welfare dependency is a New Right idea which claims that an unemployed underclass is living off the welfare state and is unwilling to work.

2 Item A provides you with the information. However, don't just copy it. Put it into your own words.

3 Any three from:

- They tend to occupy semi-skilled or unskilled jobs.
- They are subjected to discrimination.
- They are likely to be low paid.
- Jobs are likely to be insecure.
- They experience fewer promotion opportunities.

4 Note the question emphasises explanation. It is likely your response will focus on any two of the following:

- It over-generalises about the behaviour of the poor.
- The lack of evidence for such a sub-culture – see Madge and Rutter.
- The neglect of economic explanation, i.e. the fatalistic culture of the poor may be a response to economically adverse conditions, not its cause. See Lister and Beresford.

5 Note the question is asking you to use Item A and other sources. Note the word 'outline'. This is asking you to describe New Right views as opposed to evaluating such views. However, your response would benefit from contrasting New Right views with alternative explanations. Your plan should therefore look like this:

- Use Item A to show that the New Right thinkers such as Saunders see an underclass at the heart of the relationship between inequality and welfare. Supplement this with other sources, e.g. Murray. Show

how these thinkers have been influenced by Lewis' work. Outline Marsland's ideas about welfare dependency, selectivity and the private sector.

- Contrast with Jordan's ideas about universal benefits, and other sociologists who argue that most welfare claimants are trapped in economic situations beyond their control. Moreover, New Right ideas are criticised for scapegoating those on benefits.

6 Note that the question is asking you to use information from Item B and other sources. Note too the emphasis on evaluation. Your plan should look like this:

- The introduction should set the scene of the debate. The view that poverty is an inevitable feature of the way society is organised is associated with Marxist sociologists who situate poverty in the larger structure of class inequality. Weberian sociologists, too, suggest poverty is socially structured by inequalities in the organisation of the labour market.
- Outline the Marxist argument with reference to writers such as Kincaid, Westergaard and Resler, Le Grande, etc.
- Critique of Marxism. For example, it doesn't explain why some groups are more prone to poverty than others – especially women and ethnic minorities.
- Outline the Weberian argument with reference to Barron and Norris' dual labour-market theory, and Rex and Tomlinson (Item B).
- Contrast Marxism and Weberian theories briefly with the New Right view that individual fecklessness and the over-generosity of the welfare state are to blame, rather than the organisation of society.

Chapter 9 Work and leisure

This is a typical AQA question.

1 Scientific management refers to the process in which control and decision-making is taken away from workers. Jobs are studied and timed. Management sets targets and the methods of achieving these.

2 Industrial sabotage may involve the breaking of a machine such as an assembly line in order to slow it down. Strikes involve the stoppage of work until a grievance is settled.

3 Any three from:
- It involves taking power away from workers.
- Creative powers do not lie with the worker.
- Mass production usually involves isolation from other workers.
- Work may be repetitive and boring.
- Work is usually unskilled and therefore low paid.

4 Two from:
- Not all forms of industrial action are official.
- Strike action may not last long enough to constitute an official figure.
- Strikes may not be reported.
- Some types of industrial action are difficult to quantify, e.g. sabotage.

5 Note that you must make reference to the material in Item A. You must assess theories once you've outlined them. Begin by distinguishing between different types of industrial conflict; strikes, working to rule, refusal to work overtime, sabotage, etc. Theories of industrial action to be outlined and evaluated should include:
- the 'isolated mass theory' of Kerr and Siegel

- Edwards and Scullion
- Huw Beynon. This theory should be linked to Item A and assembly-line production
- Harry Braverman's theory of de-skilling implies that the resulting alienation creates the conditions for industrial action.

6 Note emphasis on 'both Items'. Evaluation must also be applied throughout. Begin with Marx who suggests that in capitalist societies only a few individuals are allowed the freedom to express themselves in their work. This is because, as Item B suggests, the organisation of capitalism has taken creative opportunities away from workers because of techniques such as Taylorism (mentioned in Item A). The capitalist class controls the labour process. As a result, work is alien to the worker. As Item B states, the worker has become a slave of the machine and management practices.

- Outline Marx's ideas. As Item B states, workers are unable to identify with the products of their labour because they only play a partial role in their production. Workers generally feel indifferent and sometimes even hostile to work. This can result in a range of industrial action.

- Contrast Marx with Robert Blauner's views. Focus on Blauner's four dimensions of alienation: powerlessness, meaninglessness, isolation and self-estrangement. Don't forget to criticise Blauner's methodology.

  Focus, too, on Gallie and Beynon and contrast with Goldthorpe and Lockwood's study of affluent workers.

Chapter 10 Health

This is a typical AQA question.

1 Infant mortality refers to the number of infants who die between birth and exactly one year of age. It is usually expressed as a rate per 1000 live births.

2 Any two from:
- the housewife role
- the mother role
- the dual burden, i.e. combining paid work and mother–housewife role
- low-skilled, low-paid employment.

3 Any three from:
- mass vaccination
- developments in surgery, especially transplant surgery
- developments in drug technology
- the National Health Service.

4 Note the emphasis on 'briefly describe'.
- Busfield (1983) notes that definitions of mental illness are relative to gender. Illustrate.
- Radical feminists argue that some definitions of illness are specifically aimed at controlling the behaviour of females. Illustrate.

5 The question is only asking for an explanation. However, a particular point of view – the biomedical view – takes credit for improved life expectancy in the UK. Therefore is is useful to outline this model and contrast it with other points of view. Your plan should look like this:
- Outline of the biomedical model of health – see Hart.

- Outline Thomas McKeown's alternative social model of health.
- Illich's critique of modern medicine.

6 Note that the question is asking you to use material from Item B and elsewhere. You need to focus on evaluation, too. This is likely to be achieved by comparing and contrasting theories. Your plan should look like this:
- Outline the differences in mortality and morbidity between men and women.

Explanations:
- Are the statistics misleading? Illustrate with reference to McFarlane.
- Do the statistics reflect gender-role socialisation? – illustrate with reference to the social constructionist argument.
- The cultural–behavioural perspective sees male and female health as a cultural product. Illustrate with regard to smoking, drinking, aggression, the breadwinner role, unemployment, etc.
- Feminist explanations focus on the nature of the mother–housewife role (Item B refers to this). Illustrate with reference to Graham and Bernard.
- Marxist-feminists focus on the poverty, low wages and unemployment experienced by some women. Illustrate with reference to single mothers, etc.

Index